KEEPING THE FAITH

BEST INDIANA SERMONS

Guild Press Emmis Books

Guild Press
10665 Andrade Drive
Zionsville, IN 46074
(800) 913-9563

www. guildpress.com

ISBN: 1-57860-130-4

Library of Congress: 2003100712

CONTENTS

INTRODUCTION

Although America is a religious nation, one of the most "practicing" among Western nations, with a high percentage of its people saying they believe in God, I am not sure every state in the union could compile such a comprehensive and representative collection of sermons as this one. Its publication is a happy correspondence of spirit and place.

The idea that a collection of excellent sermons from our state should be published was developed at Emmis Publishing, the parent corporation of Guild Press. Emmis' interest in the more significant parts of Hoosier life is attested to by the corporation's philanthropy and involvement in civic betterment. Surely commercial interest alone would not dictate the publication of a book of inspiring messages about leading a deeper, more meaningful life.

A call for sermons went out in 2002 to every county in the state through daily and weekly newspapers and many of the entries in this book from smaller towns came as a result of this call: clergy people and congregations agreed on a particularly effective sermon and sent it in for consideration. The enthusiasm for the project from the Michigan border to the Ohio River country was sincerely gratifying even if it made the final selection process difficult. Denominational headquarters and leaders were asked to pass the word along; older and famous ministers and priests submitted their best efforts as well as newly minted seminarians. Jewish, Moslem, Catholic and a variety of Protestant traditions are represented in the collection.

We who edited were surprised and delighted with the depth of thinking that is going on not only in our huge cathedrals and megachurches throughout the state, but also in small towns where there may only be one church. In spite of what seems to be rampant materialism, people are gathering, absorbing their religious traditions and going forth to lead better lives. Indiana is, indeed, a place of spirit and meaning and Guild Press is pleased to be the facilitator of the messages contained in this book. May you be inspired and uplifted, as we who worked on the project were.

Special thanks should go to Art Baxter, who patiently coordinated the project including designing and typesetting the book, and to Rev. Donald Charles Lacy and Dr. David E. Sumner who assisted in editing. Part of the proceeds from this book will go to the Indiana Gleaners Food Bank.

Nancy Niblack Baxter, President
Guild Press Emmis Books

AFTER ALL, YOU NEVER KNOW

There is an ancient Jewish legend which says the world is sustained by thirty-six righteous people (the *ilamed vavniksi*). No one knows who they are, but their acts of kindness and justice are the foundation of the earth. If one of them should die and not be replaced by another, the world could not exist. A story for the millennia.

I recently read a retelling of this legend.[1] In it a town is plagued by a lack of rain. Everyone prays—from the prominent lawyer to the beloved baker—but nothing happens. No rain. Not a trickle. Then the poor shoemaker offers to pray. People laugh, for the shoemaker is not only poor, he is foolish. He is a kind man, always there to help, but not very wise. The people call him "the stupid shoemaker." But when he prays, the rain falls. The townspeople realize that the poor shoemaker is one of the thirty-six righteous. Then he disappears. When another cobbler comes to town, the people have changed. No one calls the new cobbler "stupid." Everyone is kind to him. He could be one of the thirty-six righteous. Because after all, you never know.

These words have stayed with me ever since I read this story:

"After all, you never know." You never know what effect your deeds or your words have on another, and on the world.

When I was deciding on what to speak about these High Holy Days, I piled up stacks of books. After reading through chapter after chapter, nothing grabbed me. In desperation, I said to my husband, "I just don't know what to speak about this year." He said, "Say what is in your heart." This is what is in my heart.

In a world as fast paced as our own, where there never seems to be enough time to accomplish all that needs to be done, we are inclined to overlook people who cannot help us achieve our goals. We whisk through life with little attention to the remarks we make in passing, to our casual everyday acts.

What if we acted differently? What if we believed that every deed we performed, every word we spoke were the acts and the words which either sustained or destroyed the world? After all, you never know.

I am enough of a mystic to affirm that belief—to keep faith with the Jewish mystical tradition which tells me that everything contains within it a holy spark, from the most mundane place to the least desirable person. We find ourselves in a certain place, with particular people not by chance but to redeem the divine sparks contained therein. How we act in those spaces, with those people, will determine the world's fate. For when all the sparks are lifted up, returned to God, redemption will come.

I am enough of a mystic, a lover of poetry, to believe it, but I am also enough of a realist, a rationalist, to doubt it. Sustain the whole world by a simple embrace, a kind word—probably not. But then, I think again—perhaps. The mystics were not referring to the whole universe but to the smaller worlds we inhabit on a daily basis—our families, our businesses, our neighborhoods, ourselves. I am back again to affirming the underlying truth of the mystical cosmology and the striking legend of the thirty-six righteous. If you save one life, it is as if you saved an entire world. Because after all, you never know.

When you write a story, as I enjoy doing, you need to pay attention to the details. It matters how the table is set, the chairs are arranged; who is in the room, how the characters relate to one another. It matters if they shake hands, embrace or simply nod. Little movements speak worlds. I believe what is true in literature is true in life.

Last fall I had the opportunity to moderate a discussion with Thomas Keneally, the author of *Schindler's List*, at Clowes Hall [Butler University, Indianapolis]. He talked about how those whom Schindler helped to survive remembered him. It was not the grand salvific acts about which they reminisced, but the small acts of kindness that restored their humanity. This is what they remembered— a pair of eyeglasses made, a lit cigarette left to smoke, the gathering of a *minyan* to say kaddish. Schindler's leadership was in what Keneally called acts of sanctifying grace . . . small gestures, affirmations of humanity, redeeming the holy sparks, saving worlds.

When the Episcopal archbishop Desmond Tutu of South Africa, winner of a Nobel Peace Prize for helping to bring an end to apartheid, was asked about a formative experience in his life, he replied, "One incident immediately comes to mind. When I was a young child, I saw a white man tip his hat to a black woman. Please understand that such a gesture was completely unheard of in my country. The white man was an Episcopal bishop, and the black woman was my mother." A tip of the hat, a seemingly inconsequential gesture, was the beginning to the end of apartheid.

Many Jewish narratives remind us of the power of such acts of sanctifying grace. Eliezer, Abraham's servant, chooses Rebecca as a wife for Isaac. Why? Was it because of her exceeding beauty, her sharp intellect, her compatible beliefs? None of the above. Eliezer knew Rebecca was the right choice because when he saw her at the well, she offered him drink and his camels also. Rebecca became a matriarch of our people because she gave water to a stranger, an act of sanctifying grace.

Hillel is the revered sage of our rabbinic heritage. If we know anything from that period, we know what Hillel said. Why? Was it his grand mind, his elegant prose, his great power? He may claim all of those in part, but others were surely grander, more elegant and more powerful than he. Hillel is our most quoted sage because of his kindness. When a heathen who wished to mock the Jewish tradition came to him and insisted, "Tell me all of Judaism while I stand on one foot," Hillel did. Patient, unlike his contemporary Shammai, who had thrown the impudent man out of his study, he responded, "What is hateful to you do not do to your neighbor. This is the whole Torah. The rest is commentary. Now, go and study." Hillel treated a skeptic who had come to mock him with respect and honor—an act of sanctifying grace which probably gained a convert. People will tell me one of the primary reasons they join one synagogue over another is not because of the congregation's ideology or liturgy, but because when they come to services someone speaks to them.

The rabbis ask why the Book of Ruth was included in the Biblical canon. There is no mention of God, no teaching about ritual, no reference to law. It is simply the story of friendship between two women following personal tragedy. Why then include the narrative in the Bible? Because, say the rabbis, it speaks of *gemilut hasadim*, acts of loving kindness.

In this age of millennial speech and movies—of *Armageddon, Deep Impact* and a myriad of other cataclysmic stories and visions of the end of our century—we need to focus less on the end of time and more on this time, less on grandiose acts and more on simple ones.

Think of the words you say to others. Are they angry, cruel? Do you criticize more than you praise? Do you hold grudges more than you forgive? Are you cynical, sarcastic more than understanding?

When you leave this sanctuary, will you find fault more than you admire, will you show disdain more than respect? Consider being more forgiving, speaking words of gratitude more than complaint, because after all, you never know.

Think of the deeds you perform—no, not the big ones—the business deals you close, the cases you win, the computers you program—but the small ones. Do you cheat others and your family members of time, of love because of busy schedules? Do you offer assistance even when a person can be of no assistance to you? Do you plant a garden, smile at a child, sit with someone who is troubled or ill? Consider paying attention to the smaller gestures— bringing flowers, volunteering time for others, calling a friend. Because after all, you never know. The greatest mitzvah in Judaism is placing soil on the grave of a loved one because burying one's dead is a mitzvah for which there is no expectation of reward. What deeds do you perform for which you expect nothing in return?

Think of your Jewish commitments. There is so much written about those grand programs which will secure the future of Judaism—trips to Israel, retreats, *kallot*, camps. They are all important but devoid of a larger Jewish context; they are simply interesting experiences. Franz Rosenzweig was about to convert to Christianity when he entered a synagogue on Yom Kippur and heard the haunting chant of the Kol Nidre. He became an observant Jew and one of the foremost Jewish thinkers of modernity. It all began with a simple melody.

Consider the smaller acts. Invite someone for Shabbat dinner, tell a Jewish story to a child, read a Jewish book, study a passage of Torah, say the blessing over the bread, sit in a sukkah, march with the Torah. Consider that these acts may make a difference in our Jewish future. Because after all, you never know.

I was having lunch with a group of authors a short while before the High Holy Days. I asked for ideas for my High Holy Days sermons. "I've been writing these sermons for close to twenty-five years. What could I possibly say that is new?" Someone suggested that, in the spirit of conservation, I just recycle an old one. Attractive idea! But then another remark started me thinking—*Talk about how you have changed.*

Had I really changed? In the beginning I believed it was my role to tell you all I knew about Judaism. I came to realize that adult education classes were better suited for that kind of learning. Then I was a firm believer in tackling the political issue of the day until someone once said to me, "I don't go to synagogue to hear the Op-Ed page of *The New York Times.* I go to synagogue to learn how to put my life together, to renew my days." While I still believe there are times for teaching and discussing the issues of the day, I believe the *Yamim Noraim*, these Days of Awe are meant to figure out how to live, day-by-day, worthy lives.

There is a legend told of Rabbi Isaac Luria, the architect of much of the kabbalistic tradition. It was revealed to him that his soon-to-be-born grandson would only live a few short years. Luria asked God to give his grandson the years he had left to live, and so it was. The grandson grew up, but he was unlike his grandfather; he was renowned only for the trouble he got into, the mischief he made.

Finally, out of desperation, the father of the boy took him to the grave of the great Rabbi Isaac Luria and told him the story of how his grandfather had given him all those years of his life. Then the father asked his son, "Was it worth it?"

How would we who stand here today before the generations of our ancestors, who lived their lives so ours might be better, answer that question? Was it worth it? Are we worthy of the years—few or many—which we are given or do we waste them away? Do we weigh each deed as though it might be the one which will sustain the world, or do we act carelessly without regard for the places we inhabit or the people we meet?

The questions with which we begin our careers are different. Can we make it? Make a name for ourselves? Will we be successful? But Yom Kippur requires us to ask the more important question, "Are we worthy of the years, the days, the hours we are given?"

When I saw the movie *Saving Private Ryan* I could not help but think of the legend of Rabbi Isaac Luria. Most of the film reviews focused on the horror of the war and the honesty in which it was portrayed. Assuredly it was not easy to watch the opening twenty-five minutes of tragic detail as the troops landed on Omaha Beach of Normandy. However, the most difficult part of the film, the part no hand-over-the-eyes could shield us from, was not the blood and guts but were the words of Private Ryan as he wept before the grave of the Captain who saved his life and who had told him in the end to "Earn this. Earn it." The private, now a grown man with a family, pleads, "Tell me I have lived a good life. Tell me I have been a good man."

Sitting here in this sanctuary on the holiest day of the year surrounded by the lights of Yizkor, the memory of those who fought the wars, paved the roads, who made the homes in which we grew up, who cooked the meals we ate and washed the clothes we wore— who worked and sacrificed so we could achieve more than they ever imagined—we ask ourselves, *Was it worth it? Have we earned it?*

Tell us we have lived a good life. Tell us we have been good people.

And if we have not, if our successes leave us empty, our accomplishments unsatisfied, if we are disappointed in the way we have chosen to live, Yom Kippur tells us we can change.

Remember Schindler's acts of sanctifying grace. Remember the legend of the thirty-six righteous for whose sake the world is said to exist.

Make your everyday language, your routine deeds, worthy of your gift of life because—**After All, You Never Know**.

[1] From *You Never Know: A Legend of the Lamed-vavniks* by Franevne Prose.

Rabbi Sandy Eisenberg Sasso
Congregation Beth-El Zedeck
Indianapolis
Yom Kippur 5759

Rabbi Sandy Eisenberg Sasso earned a Bachelor of arts degree and a Master of Arts in Religion from Temple University. She earned her Doctor of Ministry degree from Christian Theological Seminary in Indianapolis. She has been rabbi of Congregation Beth-El Zedeck since 1977. She has received honorary Doctorates from Christian Theological Seminary, Depauw University, Butler University and the Reconstructionist Rabbinical College. She lectures at Butler University and is the author of many articles and children's books dealing with issues of spirituality. Her newest book is *Cain and Abel—Finding the Fruits of Peace*. She most recently edited *Urban Tapestry, Indianapolis Stories*.

Run With The Horses!

*If you have raced with foot-runners and they have wearied you,
how will you compete with horses? And if in a safe land you fall down
how will you fare in the thickets of the Jordan?*
Jeremiah 12:5

Tuesday, September 11, 2001 our fantasy world of high technology and self-sufficiency was shattered. Early that pristine morning, thousands of preoccupied men and women rode high-speed elevators to their offices high in the skies in what has been called "the electronic nerve center for the civilized world." Minutes later they were fleeing on foot down flights of endless, coiling stairs like well-dressed refugees, their cell phones clutched against their ears. As they ran for their lives, virtual money, "coursing through the computers of Morgan Stanley and Cantor Fitzgerald," began to "flutter down on Lower Manhattan in a nightmarish version of a ticker-tape parade." Meanwhile, as we sat watching those twin towers implode on live television, terror seethed in our souls as our world changed before our very eyes.

In an instant, terrible truths we had all but forgotten came back to haunt us—truths about sin and evil and the nature of life itself. We discovered that evil is real, the devil is not dead, sin lurks in every nook and cranny of life. To be human is to be vulnerable.

By day's end another and greater truth had also surfaced— we discovered that we were not alone. We sensed God was with us. God became our refuge and our hope. Amidst the terror of evil, we learned that God knows his way out of the grave! How else do you account for churches like this one filled with people in prayer by Tuesday evening? How else do you explain last Sunday dawning like Easter with standing-room-only crowds thronging sanctuaries across America?

This week I received a letter from an Indiana Supreme Court Justice containing this quotation from David McCul-lough's new biography titled *John Adams*. The year was 1779 and John Adams was off to France on a diplomatic trip to negotiate peace with Great Britain. He invited his two sons to accompany him. His elder son, a teenager, balked at the idea. That is when the boys' mother, Abigail, picked up her pen and wrote this letter to her sulking adolescent son:

> *These are the times in which a genius would wish to live. It is not in the still calm of life, or the repose of a pacific station, that great characters are formed. The habits of a vigorous mind are formed in contending with difficulties. Great necessities call out great virtues. When a mind is raised, and animated by scenes that engage the heart, then those qualities which would otherwise lay dormant, wake into life.*

Last week we were rudely awakened to both the terrible reality of evil and the eternal verities of God. In that moment faith as character was formed.

There is a power in this world called evil. As Martin Luther put it in his hymn, *A Mighty Fortress*, this evil power "seeks to work us woe." But, as Luther discovered, in this world there is an even greater power—that is the saving power of God who surprises us amidst tragedy as a presence beyond words.

Elie Wiesel tells this story. One day while he was incarcerated at Auschwitz, one of Hitler's death camps, there was a triple hanging at the hands of the German SS that all the inmates were forced to watch. It was an ugly, evil moment. Among the three persons to be hanged was a young boy. As the noose around the child's neck caught and the boy dangled blue-tinged in the light, someone in the crowd shouted: "Where is God? Where is God now?" Wiesel writes: "And I heard a voice within me answer him: 'Where is *He*? Here *He* is—hanging on this gallows.'"

Where was God on Tuesday, September 11th? I believe that God was among the passengers in those four planes. I believe that God was in those twin towers when they collapsed. I believe that God was among those police and fire fighters who rushed into that hell of mangled steel and concrete to care for the dying and the wounded. I believe this because of the Bible. In the Hebrew scriptures the Psalmist says that when the "mountains shake" and the "waters storm" and the "nations war . . . the Lord of hosts is with us!" Exactly where is God in all this mess? The Psalmist answers: "God is plump in the middle of the city! Sometimes God simply weeps with us. At other times, when life turns ugly because of evil, God comes alongside and suffers with us!"

So, what now? With troopships steaming toward the Mediterranean, the military on alert, a new Cabinet post on Homeland Security in the making, the economy in turmoil and the President promising us a long, protracted battle, how now are we to live? Will we allow evil to make cowards of us?

This morning I've come to tell you a story from the Bible concerning the prophet Jeremiah. It is somewhere between 604 BC and 598 BC and Israel is under siege. Enemy armies are poised along Israel's borders. Israel is about to be plunged into a dark age that will last nearly seventy years. Jeremiah has the prophet's eyes of insight and foresight. He sees what lies ahead and speaks but no one listens. Discouraged and worn down by the opposition, Jeremiah is ready to jettison his faith and capitulate to the coming evil when God sits him down and speaks. God says:

> *Jeremiah, if you have raced with men on foot and they have wearied you, how will you compete with horses? And if in a safe land you fall down, how will you do in the thickets of the Jordan?*

In other words, "Jeremiah, life is difficult! Evil is real! Jeremiah, if you are going to survive tough times you must dare to trust God! You must run with the horses."

In the last book of the Bible, Revelation chapters six and nineteen, there is a story of a horse race. Albrecht Durer, a German artisan of the 16th century, has recorded that horse race in a famous woodcut called *The Four Horsemen of the Apocalypse*. One horse is red and named *War*. A second horse is black and named *Famine*. A third horse named *Death* is pale green, corpse colored. War, Famine, and Death symbolize evil. On the horizon there appears another horse, a great white stallion named *Faithful and True*. And sitting atop the white horse, riding amidst the devastation of evil is none other than Jesus Christ, who comes "conquering and to conquer."

To ride with the horses is to ride, in the face of evil, with Jesus Christ. It is to live believing that God is with us no matter what. To ride with the horses is to bet life on the justice of God, for in the end God wins!

The great truth claim of the Christian faith is found in First Corinthians, chapter fifteen; it is called *resurrection*. Too often we misread the story of resurrection. To understand resurrection we must be aware of the story behind the story. Behind the story of the resurrection sits the story of the cross and a suffering Jesus. The point of the resurrection story is this: only a suffering God knows how to deal with evil. Evil is tricky as well as terrible. Evil can attack from the outside like a terrorist and kill the body. Evil can also sneak up on us from within as a virus and kill the soul. In the struggle between good and evil we don't fight evil with evil. When in the heat of the fray we are tempted to chase simple solutions and say, "we just ought to bomb the hell out of those people," we must remember this story of the cross and resurrection. Only a suffering God knows how to deal with evil. Only a savvy and suffering God can bring life out of death. As the *Creed* says, Jesus was "crucified, dead and buried." Only after he died, did God get Jesus up. On the far side of death and evil stands life, but only a suffering God can guide us there. So, with a rhetorical flourish based on this resurrection reality, Paul concludes his resurrection story, trumpeting: "So, my brothers and sisters, be steadfast, immovable, always abounding in the work of the Lord." In those words I hear Paul say: "Saddle up! Ride with the horses!"

What does it mean to saddle up and ride with the horses? Back to our Jeremiah story. Time has passed and for Jeremiah life has gone from bad to worse. Evil pelts Jeremiah's world like hail stones the size of baseballs. The king puts Jeremiah in prison in an attempt to silence him. The Babylonian army is pounding on the outside walls of Jerusalem. Inside the city, bread is so scarce that the people have resorted to cannibalism. It is only a matter of hours until the walls fall and death strikes. Then an unexpected message comes to Jeremiah in his prison cell. A farm belonging to his family in the city of Anathoth has become available to Jeremiah as the next of kin. Remember, Jerusalem is under siege, famine stalks the streets, the economy is in recession, terror shrivels the soul of every citizen. From his prison cell, Jeremiah carries out a real estate transaction. He purchases his cousin's farm. He buys a piece of property that he will most likely never see.

Why did Jeremiah do that? He did it because he wanted to invest in God's future. He believed that on the other side of death there was life. He believed that in the war with evil, God has the last word; God wins! He did it as a deliberate act of hope. To ride with the horses is to invest in God's future.

A number of years ago the psychiatrist M. Scott Peck wrote a book on evil titled, *People of the Lie*. Peck tells this story: He was talking about evil with his eight-year-old son and wanted to understand how children understand evil. "Why, Daddy," his son said, "that's easy—evil is *live* spelled backward." Suddenly Scott Peck says that he saw something that he had never seen before: "evil is whatever keeps us from living."

My friends, I think it's time we began to live again . . . time we stopped allowing the evil events of the last week to shrivel our world . . . time we bet our living on the resurrection . . . time for us to risk hope by investing in life. Jeremiah bought a farm because he believed that the future belonged to God. Tomorrow morning Edie and I will get on a plane and fly to California to visit our younger son and his family. It's time we all started flying again. It's time we began buying stocks again. It's time we bet our lives on God's future rather than the future of evil.

Run with the horses! Invest in God's future. So our President has declared war on terrorism. To succeed, this war against evil must be more than an American war. This war must link people together all across Planet Earth who are vulnerable to the evils of terrorism: Arabs, Europeans, Asians and Africans as well as Americans. Imagine—Christians and Jews and Muslims coming together to invest in God's future. As Christians, Jews and Muslims, we all pray to the same God, so why not invest in God's future together.

During the Second World War, the Oxford don C. S. Lewis wrote a book about evil. He titled his book *The Screwtape Letters* for it was a correspondence between a senior devil named Screwtape and a junior devil named Wormwood. One day Uncle Screwtape, as he called himself, writes: "My dear Wormwood, of course war is interesting. [However] I must caution you not to hope too much from a war." Why? Because amidst the chaos of war, "thousands turn . . . to the Enemy," to God. With those words Lewis is reminding us that war and evil and the sense of human vulnerability have a way of bringing us back to the realities of life and back to God.

Sitting in a meeting this week, a woman began to sob. As tears shook her composure she told how the events of September 11th had grabbed her soul. She said something like this: "God has been speaking to me in the events of the last week. God has been telling me that if I am going to live I need to get rid of the hatred in my life. I'm tired of hating people who did great evil to me. I now know that if I am going to live, I must learn to forgive; and I want to live!"

My hunch is that some of you have also allowed evil to keep you from living and you were not aware of that until last week. Some of you have been so preoccupied with investing in yourselves that you did not realize until this week how bankrupt you were. It is time for you to begin to invest in God. Some of you have never formed a partnership in life with this God we come to know in Jesus Christ. Today I invite you to run with the horses. I invite you to invest in God's future. I say: "Saddle up! Partner up with Jesus Christ!" Only Christ can guide us through the thickets of evil that lie ahead.

Run with the Horses!

Rev. William Enright, Senior Pastor
Second Presbyterian Church, Indianapolis
Sunday, September 16, 2001

William Enright has served as senior pastor of Second Presbyterian Church for more than twenty years.

He received his BA from Wheaton College, Wheaton, Illinois, the Th.M. from McCormick Theological Seminary, Chicago, and the Ph.D. from the University of Edinburgh, Scotland.

Currently a member of the Board of Directors for Lilly Endowment Inc., he also is active on various advisory boards of hospitals, foundations, and universities. His civic involvement in Indianapolis has included: serving as co-chair of the Mayor's Taskforce on Racism, member of Envisioning Indianapolis and the Police Advisory Board. In addition, he has been Vice-Chairman of the Board of Trustees of the Greater Indianapolis YMCA, a member of the Board of Directors of the Central Indiana Council on Aging, Wishard Hospital Foundation, St. Vincent Hospital Advisory Board and Hanover College Board of Trustees.

WE MUST GET HOME

Matthew 4:13-16

James Whitcomb Riley wrote a long poem called *We Must Get Home*. Here is a sampling of the verses.

We must get home-for we have been away
So long, it seems forever and a day!
And O so very homesick we have grown,
The laughter of the world is like a moan
In our tired hearing, and its song as vain,-
We must get home——we must get home again!

We must get home! There only may we find
The little playmates that we left behind, -
Some racing down the road; some by the brook;
Some droning at their desks, with wistful look
Across the fields and orchards – farther still
Where laughs and weeps the old wheel at the mill

We must get home: All is so quiet there:
The touch of loving hands on brow and hair –
Dim rooms, wherein the sunshine is made mild-
The lost love of mother and child
Restored in restful lullabies of rain, -
We must get home – we must get home again!

We must get home; and, unremembering there
All gain of all ambition otherwhere,
Rest – from the feverish victory, and the crown
Of conquest whose waste glory weighs us down—
Fame's fairest gifts we toss back in disdain—
We must get home— we must get home again!

Those of us who know something of Indiana history learned that James Whitcomb Riley's boyhood home was Greenfield. We also know that he spent much of his adult life living in Indianapolis in a home in Lockerbie Square. This was where he produced the bulk of his poetry. Different places became home for Riley at different points in his life and now several communities in Indiana lay claim to being his hometown.

I've never really thought about this, but Jesus would have probably also been considered a well-traveled man in his time. Born in Bethlehem, he soon traveled to Egypt where he spent the first years of his life. Then his family moved back to the land that they loved, to Nazareth, where he probably did most of his growing up. There he would have learned to read the Torah. There he would have learned his trade as a carpenter. There he would have felt the restlessness to follow the urging of the spirit. As an adult, when he had the opportunity and freedom to choose a place to live, he moved forty miles away to a seaside city called Capernaum. From that place he launched his new career as an itinerant preacher and healer. Capernaum became home. While he probably lived there for the rest of his life performing his best miracles and creating his best work, Capernaum doesn't get the mention it deserves as a place where Jesus lived. We speak of Bethlehem and Nazareth and what happened in those locations.

But today we are looking at Capernaum and considering some of the things that Jesus experienced in his own home. I think we will see that some of what Jesus experienced is not so different from what we want or hope will go on in our own hometowns. The idea that we're working with this morning is rather simple; if we consider ourselves to be spiritual people and followers of Christ, then our homes should reflect that influence. There are some things we should expect to see and there are some things we should expect to receive.

There are sixteen mentions of Capernaum in the Gospels and in every instance I think the passages are given a different twist when we think of Capernaum as being the home of Jesus. In bullet point form then, like the sampling of some verses from a long poem, we will look at a few of these episodes with the intent of fishing for some characteristics we would like to see present in our own homes or hometowns.

EPISODE ONE: Jesus is "getting home again" to Capernaum after a trip of preaching and teaching. A Roman military officer, a centurion, comes to him saying:

Lord my servant is lying at home paralyzed, in terrible distress. I am not worthy to have you come under my roof; but only speak the word, and my servant will be healed.

Matthew 8

On another occasion a royal official, someone not tied to Rome, but to the Jewish aristocracy, comes to Jesus with the hope he can heal his sick son. In both cases these men approach Jesus with a great deal of respect and admiration. And in both cases Jesus responds immediately with the kind of effort and energy you would expect to see among neighbors. And perhaps they were . . . neighbors. Jesus would have been well known in his hometown. Being a seaside community, there was a mix and blend of cultures. The centurion might have lived down the street. The royal official or local bureaucrat might have lived the next block over. In any event Jesus expressed that willingness to help, characterizing what we should expect to see in our neighborhoods and communities as well. And in this case the neighborliness was a concern to help those who were sick.

Maybe in a larger sense that is what Riley is longing for when he writes: *We must get home, we must! The touch of loving hands on brow and hair—Dim rooms, wherein the sunshine is made mild.* Home is a place where we put our healing powers to work so dim rooms of sickness can be brightened and enlivened by our presence.

EPISODE TWO: At some point in his career, Jesus takes stock of what has happened in some of the cities since he has visited and spread the message of the Gospel and realizes that in many ways they are still unrepentant. He is disappointed by the fact that things haven't changed. He even sees this in his own hometown and says,
And you, Capernaum, will you be exalted to heaven?
No, you will be brought down to Hades.
Matthew 11

I would imagine that most of us at some point have wondered if all our effort was for naught, and thought that perhaps everything was going straight to hell.

Gary Varvel's recent editorial cartoon in the *Indianapolis Star* showed a person more or less passed out while bellying up to a bar. The bartender is the state legislature and he's pouring another drink from a bottle labeled "gambling." The caption reads, "Nah, you don't have a drinking problem . . . let's have another . . . and another . . . and . . . "That resonates with me because I can remember when gambling was approved more than ten years ago. Politicians at the time promised it would never expand beyond scratch-off tickets and the numbers game. But every year since the legislature has poured another drink to the point where if Senate Bill 333 makes its way though the legislative maze we'll have pull-tab slot machines at pari-mutuel betting sites. Perhaps it's not so ludicrous to think that one day we'll see slot machines at our local 7-Eleven and Starbucks. Depending on your perspective you might say we are descending deeper and deeper into Hades.

While Jesus may have loved his hometown, that didn't stop him from being outspoken about its failings. And while he may have thought that things were going to hell, he didn't give up. Jesus returned to those cities including his own with the message of the Gospel again and again. In the midst of the criticism there was always the hope that one day he could feel that his own home would be exalted to heaven.

EPISODE THREE: On another occasion Jesus "gets back home" to Capernaum and after a few days the word got out that he was back in town:

> So many gathered around that there was no longer room
> for them, not even in front of the door; and he was speak-
> ing the word to them.   Mark 2

I'm not suggesting that we aren't good disciples if we don't have large crowds standing at the door to hear us speak the word. I am saying that a characteristic of a good home and a Christ influenced hometown is that it will be a place where teaching takes place and ideas are exchanged. Those teaching moments aren't limited to Jesus' own house, for in another Capernaum passage we learn that he taught in the local synagogue as well. One of the things I've observed through the years is that parents or individuals who practice Christian education at home more often than not lead and teach Christian education at their local church. We should expect to see teaching and learning in a Christ influenced home.

EPISODE FOUR: After an extended road trip Jesus and the disciples are once again "getting back home" to Capernaum.
When he was in the house he asked them, What were you arguing about on the way? But they were silent, for on the way they had been arguing with one another who was the greatest. He sat down, called the twelve, and said to them, Whoever wants to be first must be last of all and servant of all. Mark 9

Home needs to be the kind of environment where we can give and receive reminders of our place in the grand scheme of things. Home keeps us humble, keeps us real. I can remember coming back from an event where I had given a presentation to a large gathering of people. The response and the compliments served to make me pretty full of myself. But when I got home Tami handed me a bucket, shovel, and a roll of paper towels and said, "Here you are big shot, the cat made a mess in the basement." I was brought back to earth pretty fast. Again, Riley must have sensed the home as a great equalizer in that regard.

We must get home; and, unremembering there
All gain of all ambition otherwhere,
Rest – from the feverish victory, and the crown
Of conquest whose waste glory weighs us down.
Fame's fairest gifts we toss back in disdain—
We must get home—we must get home again!

Episode Five: It is to the people of Capernaum . . . to the hometown crowd . . . that Jesus gives one of the great analogies of faith. Many of those present had traveled a far distance over the choppy waters of the Sea of Galilee. Others had walked down the dusty road from Tiberius. They found him at the city docks. They are tired, covered with road dirt and hungry. But Jesus assures them he has the kind of food that will never perish and that will always be plentiful.

"Sir," they say, "give us this food always." "I am the bread
of life. Whoever comes to me will never be hungry, and who-
ever believes in me will never be thirsty."

John 6

Who among us, would never want to come home to that?

We must get home again—we must!
Our rainy faces pelted with dust
Creep back from the vain quest through endless strife
To find not anywhere in all of life
A happier happiness than blest us then . . .
We must get home—we must get home again!

Rev. John B. Wantz,
Meridian Street United Methodist Church
Indianapolis
March 3, 2002

John B. Wantz, D.Min., is an ordained minister in the United Methodist Church. He has served churches in Bloomington and Indianapolis since 1980. He attended seminary at the Iliff School of Theology in Denver, Colorado and has additional degrees from Christian Bible Seminary in Independence, Missouri, and Christian Theological Seminary in Indianapolis, Indiana.

FRANK AND ROSITA

Matthew 25: 34-40

His name was Frank. Mildly retarded, he lived in a halfway house in a large city. He didn't speak English. The only language he knew was Polish and he hadn't spoken it in years. His sole possession was an old bowling ball, which sat perched upon his dresser in the halfway house. His was a lonely existence.

Along came Rosita, a woman of Puerto Rican extraction. She met Frank at his halfway house. "What can I do for him?" Rosita wondered. "There must be something?" Rosita noticed something about Frank that no one had in many years—his old bowling ball. She took Frank, and his old bowling ball, and introduced him to her cousin. Rosita's cousin managed a bowling team and she thought maybe he could use Frank. He said he'd try. And that's how Frank became the seventh man on a Puerto Rican bowling team.

Frank began to come out of the shell he had lived in for many years. He began to see the team as the family he didn't have. He even began to speak again. Quite a bit, even. Not Polish, either. No, now he spoke Spanish. Frank had rejoined the living.

What made the difference? What was it that brought life to a previously lifeless man—a man who had been breathing, but was not fully alive? It was Rosita, a person who took time to get to know him; something professional caseworkers and others never had. Rosita focused on Frank and his bowling ball because she knew it was time to quit judging people by what they weren't and start concentrating on what they were. She chose to look for Frank's seemingly hidden "full"-ness, rather than his obvious emptiness. Rosita was not a professional pastor. She wasn't a Sunday school teacher or Bible study leader. So far as I know, she had no formal connection with any organized religious movement or church. What Rosita was was a member of a group that wanted to see its community, Logan Square, revitalized. She wanted to see her community come back to life after many years of neglect. Instead of devising programs or finding funding, she and the others of her group decided to make their community better from the bottom up, starting with their neediest neighbors. They felt that if they took care of the "least of these" the community would grow stronger and better. And it has.

I didn't get this true-life story out of a book of sermon illustrations. Nor did I hear it at a pastor's conference. Rather it was presented at a regional gathering of United Way staff people. It was part of a seminar on the subject of capacity building. Put briefly, capacity building's central themes are those of community and gifts concepts not normally associated with supposedly secular undertakings such as United Way. In capacity building, community means formal and informal groups and organizations and not geographical boundaries. To apply that to our town, this community is composed of things like the Lions, Kiwanis and other service clubs, this church and others, banks, stores and other centers of commerce, PTAs, schools, the university and on and on and on. It is not lines on a map. The idea of gifts is that we need to define things by their strengths, their capacities, not their weaknesses or faults.

As I sat in this meeting, hearing how capacity building could build better neighborhoods, I began to reflect on whether or not it could be applied to the church. And I began to ask myself, is the church in the capacity building business? Should it be? My answer was yes. Here's why.

Jesus was in the capacity building business. As he is our leader, we need to take on his way of seeing things, rather than the way we usually do.

We, even those of us who go to church, tend to see things as unremittingly deficient. That is, we see things in terms of what they lack, instead of what they have. We see the problems, not the potential.

This goes for how we see people, too. Even ourselves. Especially as we age. We define ourselves by the things we used to be able to do that we cannot do any longer.

You see, Jesus saw people as half full, not half empty. The old saw about the difference between how an optimist and a pessimist view the same glass has more than a little bit of truth to it. But we tend to see ourselves as if we were completely empty instead of half-full.

Jesus, on the other hand, focuses on the full part. He sees our capacity to do the sort of ministry that is not dependent upon physical or even mental prowess, the ministry of kindness or cheerfulness or goodness. He defines us, and challenges us to define ourselves, by what, with God's help, we can be.

What further proof do we need of that than his choosing of that motley crew we now know as the disciples? He didn't choose the finest religious minds of his day. Why did he pick fishermen, tax collectors and the like rather than skilled seminarians and congregational leaders? Because he saw the disciples not for what they were *not*, but for what they were *becoming*. He saw them as possessing both present and potential gifts. And he worked at helping them to see those assets. Assets they would need if they were to carry the gospel into the further reaches of their world. Jesus didn't just do this with the disciples. He does this today.

Back to Rosita and Frank. Rosita reconnected Frank to the community by getting to know him. Instead of seeing him as deficient (and Frank's deficiencies were pretty obvious to most people) she chose to see him as a friend. And that is how Christ sees us as His gifted friends. If we are honest, we know we are Jesus' friends not because we possess any special qualifications or theological training, weightlifting ability, speed or endurance. We are Jesus' friends if we do what he commands us, which our scripture lesson says consists of "feeding the hungry, clothing the naked, visiting the prisoner"—all of which mean simply being ministers of hospitality. Sometimes we minister to the least of these. Sometimes we *may be* the least of these. In all times, Jesus sees us as gifted and capable, even when no one else (not even ourselves) does.

Jesus is Rosita to our Frank.

Vaya con Dios.

J. Brent Bill, Pastoral Minister
Friends Memorial Church, Muncie (1997-2001)
Delivered at Westminster Village, Vespers Service, Muncie
March 11, 2001

J. Brent Bill is a recorded Friends (Quaker) minister who serves as the Associate Director of the Indianapolis Center for Congregations. He is also the assistant book review editor of *Friends Journal* and adjunct instructor at Earlham School of Religion. Educated at Wilmington College and Earlham School of Religion, Bill has served pastorates at Friends Memorial Church and Jericho Friends Church in Indiana and First United Methodist Church in Hillsboro, Ohio. He is the author of thirteen books (including *2002's Imagi-nation and Spirit: A Contemporary Quaker Reader*) and numerous articles and short stories. He and his wife, Nancy, live in Plainfield, Indiana.

THE PEACE OF CHRIST

Poverty, chastity and obedience are vows of religious life. But they weren't the first vows in existence. They are "Johnnies-come-lately," so to speak. They only appeared around the twelfth and thirteenth centuries. The first vow in religious life, long before those, was the vow of conversion. Cardinal Newman says, "To live is to change. To have changed often is to have become perfect. It may be otherwise in another world, but in this world that's the way it is."

Many times we seem to know about conversion because we see so many people we believe should be changing. But we don't know much about conversion in reference to ourselves. In this way, we disagree with Jesus. He tells us about a particular area in which we will disagree with him for sure. It's an area that's extremely important to us, because in this particular case we are either going to go our way or His. If there is good will in us, we are going to constantly go His way, of course as we change.

What is that area in which we have such a hard time with Jesus, such a hard time that most of our prayer is against His will? It is something we need most of all to go on. We need peace within us. Don't we say, "If I am at peace, I can take anything?" Certainly we do. But then, what is our idea of peace and how does it compare to His idea of peace? He indicates in several ways that on this particular issue we are on different wave lengths.

But there have been those who have caught on to His way of thinking and change. They are the only successful people. They are the saints. All through their lives they tackled this problem, they struggled with it and only gradually did they succeed. If we are not on the road to sanctity as they were, if we are just wallowing in our way of life, we are not moving as we should be. And finding the true peace as Jesus taught it is part of moving, of living that life of change, of conversion.

Now let's talk about peace as Jesus understands it. Let's talk about peace as we understand it. Let's talk about the successful people who caught onto His way.

Jesus says, "Peace I give you. My peace." It's not the peace the worldly person seeks. He also says, "I don't come to bring peace. I come to bring the sword." Peace and the sword? We are quick to say, "Jesus contradicts himself." Wait a minute! It's better to say, "He must be saying something we don't understand." Jesus doesn't contradict himself.

Evidently what Jesus is saying is, "I come to bring peace, but with MY peace the sword is connected. With MY peace suffering is connected." He goes on to say, "I have come to set son against father. I have come to set daughter against mother." He's saying, "I've come to cause disturbance within the family." (You know, the only one we seem to remember and concentrate on is "I have come to set daughter-in-law against mother-in-law.")

When we think of peace, the worldly way of thinking is a peace without a sword, without difficulties, without troubles.

You and I connect the idea of peace with an "if." "If I didn't have this arthritis, if I didn't have this cancer, if I didn't have this crippling condition, I would be at peace." In this way we are equating peace with good health. Jesus never promised good health or living on this earth forever. The people Jesus cured—where are they? Dead! Those healed through the ages by the power of Christ through ministry—where are they? Dead! How do we die? Ill health takes us usually. We aren't getting out of this life alive. We grow old. We grow weary. We grow feeble. And someway in all of that, we've got to find the peace that is in Jesus.

Now let's bring back one of those successful people I spoke about earlier, those who understood peace which we need as we move forward in Christian living. There was a man who walked the streets of Rome. He was known for his marvelous humor, as funny as he could be and also a practical joker. His writings are interesting and he did know suffering. For three years he couldn't keep milk on his stomach. The man lived long before the invention of Maalox. I say he had terrible ulcers but I contend he still had the peace of Christ! I'm speaking of St. Philip Neri.

Let's bring another one back. There was a fellow early on who lived in a cave all by himself. Aren't there days when we all wish we could live in a cave? People took care of him, brought him food, gave him everything he needed. But then a group came to him and said, "Come out of that cave and teach us and be our authority. We want you to lead us to God. You know the way. Please, please, please." He came out of that cave and started monastic life in the West. And it wasn't long until those very people who had begged him to come lead them wanted to get rid of him and offered him a glass of wine with a bit of poison in it. If it wasn't for the fact that that glass broke, he would have taken it. And who was that man? Benedict of Nursia. St. Benedict, our Holy Father.

I want to offer the opinion that Benedict of Nursia wasn't a dumb bunny. He knew his former followers were offering him poison, but he still had the peace of Christ, so he could endure it.

Some people say, "If only my brothers and sisters would accept me, I would be at peace. If only my group (or workplace) would understand me, I would be at peace. They need to recognize I want to contribute and I have a gift for it, but they pass me by. And so they destroy my peace." People who take this stand equate peace with family or work or group acceptance, but Christ never promised acceptance. "I have come to set son against father." What about that strange passage in the New Testament where the clan comes to collect Him because He was giving a bad name to the family? He didn't have family acceptance. And certainly the group didn't accept Him; they crucified Him.

Another returnee from the past is a young man who wanted to become a priest. His father said, "Nobody in this family becomes a priest. You become a lawyer." But after he became a lawyer, he became more convinced than ever that his Father in heaven had more to say than his father on earth and he became a priest. He was never, never allowed back in his family. He founded a religious community and when he died he was even exiled from his own religious community. Who is this man? His name is Alphonsus Liguori, the founder of the Redemptorists. He was rejected and exiled twice but I believe he had the Peace of Christ.

Others of us say, "If only they would stop lying about me, ruining my reputation, I'd be at peace." Did Christ have a good reputation? What did they say about Him? "He has his power from the Devil!" He said, "I'll give you My flesh to eat, My blood to drink." "This man is crazy," they said. That's not a good reputation.

The people who whine, "We would be at peace IF" are as worldly as the day is long. We're all sometimes whiners in that category.

Bring another one back. A woman was out to get this fellow, by hook or crook. She tried crook and became pregnant. She accused the fellow of having fathered her child. Her hope was that he would be put out of the community and realize how much she loved him and go away with her. He was put in prison until the woman could no longer stand the lie. This was Gerard Majella, the patron of mothers. Gerard Majella experienced prison, but he had the Peace of Christ.

This Peace of Christ—if you can know ulcers and prison and exile and still have it, then what is it? And is it worth anything? St. Augustine tells us what it is. He calls it *tranquillitas ordinis*. It is the tranquility we have inside when we live in the right order. What is that right order? It is simple to explain. God is God and I am not God. And because this is true, His will is supreme. Now this God is my Father, and His fatherhood is that from which all fatherhood on earth comes. What is he concerned about? He is concerned about getting us to the land where we can live forever. He is concerned about eternal life.

St. Teresa of Avila says, "We don't build our house on a bridge." We are on a bridge, so it doesn't really matter what happens here if we get THERE. If we have everything here and all our gifts fulfilled and don't get there, what's that? Christ doesn't come to make life easy. Christ comes to make us great. What does He promise? He promises us HIS Peace.

What else does he promise? HIS cross. "If you take up your cross everyday and follow Me, you are My disciples indeed." Therese of Lisieux says, "A day in the life of a Carmelite without suffering is a wasted day." Jesus promises us His cross! Every day! It isn't a cross we can choose. It's a cross He chooses to send or allow.

Oh, we are manipulators! It's that "if" again. "I could carry the cross IF it were this one." The story that's told is a little silly but to the point. A fellow said to the Lord, "This cross doesn't fit me." And He said, "Go into the cross room and stay there as long as you want until you find the right one." And so the fellow was in there a long time and came out and said, "Now I have it!" And the Lord said, "Wait a minute, that's the one you had when you went in." Don't we know that the Eternal Galilean is a carpenter? He fits the right cross to our shoulders.

You know, I personally have given lots of retreats to Mother Teresa's sisters and to Mother Teresa of Calcutta herself. And one day, sitting in New York, hearing Confessions, somebody went to Confession and came out and pulled me by the scapular. It was Mother Teresa. She said to me, "Now you know what all the foolish people don't know—what a sinner I am."

The reason we want it our way is that we are all sinners. But the connection we have with Jesus is that he is the Redeemer and Savior. He has to change our thinking, to move us along. He does this in the manner of His own approach to sin. He took all of our sin on Himself through the cross. That's what he shares.

Nothing is perfect. Perfect means *per facere*—"made all the way through." You're not made all the way through yet. I'm not made all the way through yet. But these people we talked about—they are made all the way through. They weren't made that way until they stepped across into eternal life. So there is nothing perfect here. No perfect peace here. The peace the Lord gives is enough to sustain us, no matter what crosses he shares.

Where is Philip Neri now? He has eternal health.

Where is Benedict? He's drinking the wine that overflows at the heavenly table.

Where is Gerard Majella? He has the full freedom of the children of God.

Where is Alphonsus Liguori? He's in the bosom of Abraham.

But that's to come—that ain't here, as they say.

Cardinal Newman says, "The doctrine of Christ Crucified is the only spring of real virtue and piety, and the only foundation of peace and comfort."

Dante says it all in one sentence *In voluntate eius pax nostra*—"In HIS will is our peace. Not ours." The peace of Christ is the ability to carry our cross well. If we are carrying our cross well, we are experiencing the peace of Christ.

Thomas à Kempis says, "There is no other road to true inward peace but the road of the Cross."

Charles de Foucauld was a roustabout who did everything tryable. All of a sudden he thought he'd better convert. He writes of this and starts out by saying, "What could be meant by a peace which is not like that which the world wants?" And then he answers, "It is a peace stronger than suffering. It's not a peace without warfare, but it is a peace despite warfare. Beyond warfare." He says, "It is the peace of the soul that through love has come to dwell entirely in heaven, to share heaven's own peace, regardless of anything earthly that can happen to it."

You know, I think that's what Teresa of Avila means when she says, "All the way to heaven is heaven."

St. Paul of the Cross, the Founder of the Passionists, said, "Truly, sickness is a God-given grace. It makes us discover who we are." What do we discover? We are totally dependent. Until we discover that, who are we? Pretenders.

St. Dorotheus writes, "The man who finds fault with himself accepts all things cheerfully—misfortune, loss, disgrace, dishonor and any kind of adversity. He believes he's deserving of all these things. And nothing can disturb him." No one could have more peace than this man. He says, "Oh, I have it. I'm supposed to have it. This is what's supposed to happen." There is no such thing as chance from the view of the Providence of God.

Walter Percy, the American writer, had an uncle who wrote a moving poem about how we move on as Christians through the crosses of life to the peace of God.

They Cast Their Nets in Galilee

Young John, who trimmed the flapping sail
Homeless in Patmos died.
Peter who hauled the teeming net
Head down, was crucified.

The peace of God, it is no peace
But strife closed in the sod.
Yet brothers, pray for but one thing
The marvelous peace of God.

It's His. May you have it as yours.

Amen.

Rt. Rev. Lambert Reilly,
Saint Meinrad Archabbey
100 Hill Drive
St. Meinrad

The Right Reverend Lambert Reilly, OSB, was elected Archabbot of Saint Meinrad Archabbey in 1995 by his Benedictine confreres, being the eighth abbot and fifth archabbot in the monastic community's one-hundred forty-seven-year history.

Archabbot Lambert earned a Bachelor's degree in Philosophy from St. Vincent College Latrobe, PA., in 1955. He holds a Master of Divinity and Master of Religious Education degrees from Saint Meinrad School of Theology and a Master of Science in Education from Duquesne University. He has taught Latin and education courses and has served as principal of St. Elizabeth High School, Pittsburgh, PA., and served as a consultant to the Diocese of Peoria's Office of Education.

For more than forty years, Archabbot Lambert has served as a retreat director and speaker on issues of spirituality and prayer.

JUST DANCE

Our Old Testament lesson brings to us a bit of the saga of King David. When 2 Samuel opens, King Saul of the Israelites has just died. Then in chapter 2, David is lifted up as the new King of Judah. When we meet David later in chapter 6, David has captured Jerusalem and defeated the Philistines. So now the Ark of the Covenant is being brought to Jerusalem. David is seeking to establish his rule and give the Ark a fitting home. Not only will Jerusalem be a political capital, but it will be a religious one as well.

King David is an interesting character. His name means "Beloved," and he begins his life in Bethlehem as the youngest of eight brothers. He was a shepherd boy, a boy who quickly showed great musical talent, and a boy who eventually grew up to help reunite the people of Israel after King Saul's death.

But interestingly enough, one of the things David is most famous for is his dancing. David danced. After David had secured Jerusalem, the Ark of the Covenant was brought to the city. One of David's immediate responses was to create a wonderful celebration of music. And then it happens—dancing.

When those who were carrying the ark of the Lord had taken six steps, he sacrificed a bull and a fattened calf. David, wearing a linen ephod, danced before the Lord with all his might, while he and the entire house of Israel brought up the ark of the Lord with shouts and the sound of trumpets.
[NIV, 2 Samuel 6:13-15.]

I often wonder when we lost this. I wonder when we lost that sense of dancing before the Lord. We don't often dance in our hearts and praise Him and enjoy His presence with exuberance, let alone give our bodies the freedom to dance. When did we—either as individuals or as the Church—lose the joy that bubbles up and frees us to dance with our bodies or with our emotions in celebration of our faith?

When you think about it, some of the "whys" of why we don't dance can be thought of rather quickly. There are many reasons why we don't dance before the Lord and celebrate our faith with much passion.

The first might be fear of being inappropriate. That certainly seems valid to me. No one wants to come before the Lord and do something that's not in keeping with what we're supposed to be doing. David is a perfect example of the perils of holy dancing. In verse 16 of the sixth chapter of 2 Samuel, Michal, daughter of Saul, was watching David from her window. "And when she saw King David leaping and dancing before the Lord, she despised him in her heart" (NIV, 16b). Later, Michal expresses her disgust to David—"How the king of Israel has distinguished himself today, disrobing in the sight of the slave girls of his servants as any vulgar fellow would!" (NIV, 20b). Pretty strong stuff! Michal isn't shy about voicing her opinion on how inappropriate David was. But was it really a matter of David being vulgar and disrobing? There isn't much evidence to that effect. Nothing in the verses state that David threw off his linen garment while dancing. It would seem that this daughter of Saul was overcome not by disgust, but by her own pride. She couldn't cope with a king who could possibly be so "undignified." She was blind to the truth—David was a man passionately in love with God. His way of expressing his love and his joy was pure and true. And it was something that the world had a little trouble understanding. Sounds as true today as it was then.

Then there's embarrassment. What might people think? What in the world would people think of me if I got a little too passionate in my faith? What if my toes start tapping? What if my heart starts leaping? What if I look too enthusiastic in my faith journey?

I had a very special pal in seminary. He was a first-year student, just like me. And there was something about him that made it kind of hard not to smile when he came around. You see, he had a zest for life. He was an English major in college, and he carried that love of literature and learning with him into seminary. I know English majors are not known for being crazy and wearing lampshades on their heads, but this guy was different. He would read a book like you would savor a dessert. The words seemed to leap off the page for him, and when an idea was particularly exciting for him, he had to stop reading and share it aloud. I almost fell off my chair when I found out he was part of a band in college. The band was called Disco Prophets. I asked him why they picked that particularly silly name. He said it just sounded cool. And his face lit up whenever he played his tape of their musical antics.

I remember another time spent with this friend that just made me want to laugh out loud. We were at a stoplight, and there was a sign that said we needed to pull forward to a particular spot so that the signal would be activated and we'd get a green light. "Isn't that amazing?" he said. "We have technology that allows us to affect stoplights just by pulling our cars up to a certain point. Isn't that cool?" Well, I'd never really thought about it before. I had to smile because the amazing thing was not the traffic technology, but this person's ability to find wonder and joy at every turn. It was easy for me to think his enthusiasm was a bit weird sometimes, and maybe it was. But it was a wonderful kind of weird. This person had a zest for life—the kind of zest we're challenged to have in our daily walk of faith. When was the last time we allowed ourselves to stop and applaud a sunset? When was the last time we allowed a prayer or a spiritual song to move us to tears? What we're called to is not a faith life of pure drama for drama's sake, but a faith life of authenticity and emotional, spiritual richness. We need to give ourselves permission to experience more fully the love of God. We need to give ourselves permission to immerse ourselves in that love. We need to give ourselves permission to dance.

But maybe the problem is not permission, but burden. Maybe you're sitting here today with the desire to dance but the weight of a two-ton truck is on your shoulders. There's no way to reach the dance floor because of the anvils on your back.

Well, the truth is, we are called to cast that burden upon God. So often we hoard pain for ourselves, pain that we need to relinquish to God. Sometimes we need to give it over to God again and again. Sometimes relinquishing that burden is a process that takes time. But we need to do it. "Come to me, all you who are weary and burdened, and I will give you rest. Take my yoke upon you and learn from me, for I am gentle and humble in heart, and you will find rest for your souls" [NIV, Matthew 11:28-29]. Through Jesus, we know God is waiting to unburden us as many times as we need. Not only does this enable us to dance, but this help from God is reason to dance in itself.

But there's another unfortunate obstacle to dancing. So often, we don't believe we're entitled to a spin on the dance floor. We feel crushed and squashed like a bug. Not only do we feel incapable of dancing, but we feel the world has taken away our dance card and ripped it to shreds. Recently, I had a truly horrible experience. I was having some difficulty thinking through a troubling problem. I called someone for advice, a person whom I thought could give me an objective, expert opinion. Instead, what I heard on the other end of the phone was a series of insults. Apparently my struggle with this problem was the most ludicrous thing they had ever heard of, and they felt they had the right to use hurtful language to let me know how completely ridiculous I was being. I can't remember the last time I was made to feel so utterly worthless and beyond hope.

After I hung up the phone, my mind was reeling, and I eventually sat down at my desk. I don't think anyone has ever made me feel that way in my entire life. With tears streaming down my face, I started saying a prayer, hoping that I could start to make sense of what had happened. Then a picture formed in my mind. It was God, cradling my head in His arms. He was gently stroking my hair as if to let me know that everything would be all right and that He loved me. I'm not yet sure all the lessons I am to learn from that whole experience, but I do know that God did not create us to have our spirits squashed like bugs. We are meant to dance. Cruel, hateful, evil things are going to come into our lives. They are going to find their way in, even over the phone. These things are going to tell us we're worthless and alone and lost. But we are created to leap and dance before the Lord because it is He who loves us. If we want to find eternal love—unconditional love—we have to look to Him. Yes, Christians are to be the hands and feet of God and witnesses to God's love. But it is only God *Himself* who can give us true, eternal, unconditional, no-holds-barred, come-as-you-are kind of love. *That is our call to the dance floor.* What I invite you to do this morning is *not* to change your personality. God made some of us to be quiet and introspective. He made others to be loud and boisterous. But whatever your style, know that you are invited to the dance floor. You are invited to leap with faith, to twirl in holy happiness. David gave us that example as he danced with joy to celebrate the arrival of the Ark of the Covenant and to celebrate the love that God had showered upon him. Feel free to jump and sway and celebrate, whether it be in the pews or in your hearts. When God creates stanzas of joy in your life, just dance.

If I were in heaven,
I would play my harp,
and sing songs of praise with the angels.
If I were in heaven, I would dance with joy, and fill the air with
laughter.
Let earth be like heaven, and people like angels;
Let all sing songs of praise.
Don't wait to die, enjoy heaven now;
Don't argue or cavil—just dance.[1]

---

[1]"Heaven Now" from *Celtic Praise, The Interpreter's One-Volume Commentary on the Bible*, other references from *Nelson's New Illustrated Bible Dictionary*, *735 Baffling Bible Questions Answered*, *NIV Spiritual Formation Bible*, *Nelson's New Illustrated Bible Manners & Customs*.

Rev. Lisa Marchal
Rockdale United Methodist Church
West Harrison
July 16, 2000

Lisa Marchal is a commissioned, probationary member of the South
Indiana Conference and has pastored since June, 1999. She graduated from
Indiana University (BA, 1996) and Methodist Theological School in Ohio
(MDiv., 1999). She currently pastors Rockdale United Methodist Church in
West Harrison, Indiana. Previously, she served as Director of Christian Edu-
cation at Westerville Community United Church of Christ in Westerville, Ohio,
and as Youth Coordinator at Fairview United Methodist Church in Bloom-
ington, Indiana. She also served as a student intern at Wesley's Chapel and
Leysian Mission in London, England, during the summer of 1997.

STUDENTS AND SUFFERING

Whenever I am asked to reflect on the difficult subject of human suffering, my mind travels quickly back to a letter I received from a friend of mine early on during my years in the seminary. His mother had died about six months before he wrote to me, and he had been constantly at her side during the final months of her painful ordeal with cancer. Her illness and death threw him into a funk—a really dark mood—and he seemed to be drifting and suffering. That, at least is how it seemed to me, and I had written telling him of my love and concern for him but also encouraging him to re-focus and to re-engage his work and so forth.

He replied to me, and I still have the letter he wrote. He responded kindly to my somewhat insensitive words to him and told me how he was doing. In the course of his letter, he addressed the matter of how he and I confronted suffering—at least as he saw it. This is what he wrote:

> Besides, our outlooks on life are diametrically opposed—you still retain hope for bettering the world, I don't. You see your task as that of alleviating suffering; I see my task as sharing in suffering. I don't believe one is right and the other

*wrong— both are necessary parts of reality. It just seems to
me that whatever we do suffering remains, and just as important as reducing suffering is the ability to understand
suffering.*

My friend's words left a mark upon me, and I have thought
about them over the years since. As my own direct experience and
knowledge of suffering has grown during this time, I have come
to see that one should not make too much of the distinction between alleviating suffering and sharing in it. The two tend to be
related in my experience in ways that are difficult to describe.

Now I cannot tell you that I have endured a lot of suffering.
But my life has intersected with those of young men and women
who have suffered deeply in ways beyond the normal teenage angst
or post-college blues. Rather strangely, one sometimes hears the
comment that "students know little of suffering." Of course, this
remark is usually uttered by those who don't really know students.
They don't know of the young woman trapped by the deep unhap-
piness of her childhood or of the young woman so psychologically
troubled that she destroys her own body. They neither know of the
young man whose father was ripped from him by a tragic car accident nor of the young man who hides his grief and pain at the
breakup of his parents' marriage behind his guarded and cynical
exterior.

In fact all of us know what suffering is to some extent or other.
It is unquestionably part of our human condition. It might result.
from fissures in our families. It might be shabby treatment from
those whose friendship and trust we yearn for. It might involve the
fatigue and frustration in our studies and seeing the crumbling of
our carefully made academic plans—those painful realizations that
we are not going to be doctors or engineers. It might come in being

rejected for the nice position or good graduate program on which our heart was set. It might come through the experience of loneliness and homesickness or in observing the pain and distress in the lives of others and being pretty helpless to do much about it. Suffering is part of every life and is to be expected in our own.

What should we do? Suffering can't be explained away. It is too real for that. But could we deny it? Perhaps for a time, but only to our ultimate cost. Should we simply endure it? Perhaps at times the "grin and bear it" approach is all we can muster, but it is hardly the best long-term approach. I want to suggest that in the end we must accept the suffering that comes and use it. This is hard to explain and even harder to do. But we must not let suffering push us to withdraw or let it embitter and harden us. Rather we should see in suffering a means to become more open to the suffering of others. Through experiencing pain ourselves we can become like my dear friend and be much more able to empathize with others and to help them in their need.

My fellow Holy Cross priest, Fr. John Dunne, in his marvelous book *The Church of the Poor Devil*, maintains that "it is willingness to suffer that enables us to love." The suffering can shape and mold us to be more willing to give of ourselves to others not out of some kind of noblesse oblige but out of a recognition that we are wayfarers on a common journey who need to support each other along the way. We should take Jesus as our model, the very one who was willing to drink the cup he was poured and given, difficult though that was. We must, with God's help, do the same.

Some years ago I visited a place of sadness and terrible tragedy—the small southeast Asian nation of Cambodia, or Kampuchea. This country's recent history has been simply horrendous, as you might know. The Vietnam War spilled over its borders and half of the country was bombed by B-52s, causing death, injuries and great disruption. Then in 1975 Pol Pot and the vicious Khmer Rouge came to power. They began a virtual genocide on the Cambodian people. In acts of dastardly madness they began to kill off teachers and doctors and civil servants—anyone with education. They tried to destroy religion and traditional Cambodian culture. They drove people from the cities to the countryside, and there was mass starvation. In all, over a million people were killed and the whole infrastructure of the country destroyed. Eventually Pol Pot was forced out and has since died. But the country he so brutalized still hobbles along trying to regain some real stability and peace.

During my visit to Cambodia I visited Tuol Sleng prison in Phnom Penh, a horrible torture chamber where ordinary men and women were subjected to unspeakable acts of brutality. I saw Cheong Ek, one of the "killing fields," a site of mass graves containing the remains of literally hundreds of Cambodians. It was very troubling and moving all at once. But the most poignant episode during my stay occurred on a visit to the National School of Music and Dance. There I observed a group of elderly ladies, who somehow or other had survived the horrors of Pol Pot, instructing young girls in traditional Cambodian dance. They were reclaiming and rebuilding their decimated culture in a very tangible way. The sadness and pain of the old ladies was deeply etched in their faces, but it did not prevent them from generously and gently passing on to the eager and happy little girls their treasured knowledge of the beautiful dance which brings such joy and delight to the Cambodian people. On one level it was a small thing. On another I took it as a marvelous sign of the capacity of the human spirit to survive and to struggle on despite of suffering.

Christians have as their guide and model Jesus, the suffering servant. He knows of our pain and suffering first-hand experience and walks beside us in our times of distress. His support can help us bear the heaviest of burdens and not be paralyzed by them. Accepting suffering, sharing it, and working to alleviate it are all related aspects of the deep hope that comes from knowing that Jesus is the very one who suffered and died for us.

Rev. Wilson D. Miscamble, C.S.C.

Fr. Miscamble is a Holy Cross priest and a professor of American history at the University of Notre Dame. Born in Roma, Australia, Fr. Miscamble came to the United States in 1976 and was ordained in 1988. He has received numerous teaching awards and has written extensively on American foreign policy.

This sermon is reprinted with permission by Ave Maria Press from *Keeping the Faith, Making a Difference*, by Wilson D. Miscamble, C.S.C., Holy Cross priest at the University of Notre Dame.

Humbug!

Scripture: John 3:16—17; John 14:1—7

The advertisement arrived in the mail unexpectedly—"Come tour our family resort center and win one of three great prizes—a car, a family vacation in Florida, or a La-Z-Boy chair." Wow, I thought. How could a person go wrong? The worst I could do was a new La-Z-Boy chair for the family room!

The rules indicated that everyone in a family had to be present to win. So, the whole family drove to the location and took the tour. At its conclusion, and after I had declined a membership costing several thousand dollars per year, the salesman indicated I had won the chair. Well, I consoled myself, it isn't a car, it isn't a free stay at Disney World, but it *is* a new chair. They told me to bring my vehicle around to the pick-up dock, and once there, they handed me my "La-Z-boy chair"—a small, steel frame, canvas-backed stadium seat fine for viewing football games! But where was my big, comfy, La-Z-Boy family room chair, complete with reclining feature and pop-up footrest, which my mind had been led to conjure?

I had been duped; I had been "taken." It *did* say "Made by La-Z-Boy" on the back of the chair, but the chair hardly lived up to its billing. The promo, the hype, the advertised "glitter" made it seem as if something really nice, worthwhile—even wonderful—was coming my way. In truth, it was different, disappointing, certainly not deserving my time and effort, and definitely not worth a two-hour drive to the resort center!

My family thought it was incredibly funny. I was less amused, less capable of hilarity, glee and laughter. Bah, humbug, I thought. Humbug!

In his dictionary, Daniel Webster indicates that, as a noun, the term "humbug" refers either to a person who was a charlatan or an imposter or to the hoax or fake that such a person perpetrated. And "humbug," as a verb, refers to tricking or cheating someone.

When Scrooge in Charles Dickens' *A Christmas Carol* condemns the Christmas spirit and the Christmas season as "humbug," he means that they are nonsense, rubbish. Through the eyes of the cynical Scrooge, Christmas is a hoax perpetrated by Christians, who are out to "trick" the public. Christmas is all *glitter* and no gold . . . pretense and no substance, appearance and no reality. It's all phony, it's all fake, it's all *humbug*.

I suppose, I confess, there is a smidgen of truth to this. Sometimes during this Christmas time of the year, people who do not like each other are momentarily nice to each other; some drivers—the same ones that earlier in the year would have smashed and crashed you if you had nosed your car out in front of them, courteously let you proceed ahead of them in mall parking lots; people on the street seem friendlier, and even complete strangers put forth a faint smile when encountered.

But, of course, this is not lasting. It persists only a little while! It can be deceptive if one concludes that the hearts and minds and souls of shoppers, drivers and citizens have been transformed forever by the advent of the spirit of the Christmas season!

At the same time, there does come to us in this season a glimpse of the way things *should* be, a fleeting reflection of how we *could* relate to one another. What if the Christmas spirit was lasting and contagious and convincing and transforming?

Two thousand years ago, in a faraway place, in an inconsequential backwater of the Roman Empire, a baby was born. He was not born in luxury, but in a stable; his head was not placed on satin and lace, but on hay which livestock ate; his earthly mother and earthly father were engaged, but not yet married; his mother's birthpangs were suffered not in the midst of family and friends in Nazareth, but in Bethlehem during a journey to pay taxes.

And yet, there was some pretty spectacular advertising: Some Gentiles (foreign astrologer-priests called magi) came by, having determined through a bright star in the eastern sky that something important—something certainly astrological, perhaps even *astronomical*—was happening. And, following "angelic epiphany" in their fields, some ruffians from the lower echelon of Jewish society appeared in order to checkout what was happening. "Shepherds" they were called.

And paranoid King Herod so feared a potential Jewish usurper who would take away his power, that he had all the male babies slaughtered *en masse*.

Of course, you and I have the advantage of hindsight. We know how the story developed. We know how things turned out. The baby born in a manger in a nation the same size as Yellowstone National Park "grew in wisdom and stature and in favor with God and others." He was tempted like you and me. He gathered a band of disciples, as did other "rabbis" or "teachers" of his time, and he taught and "went about doing good." He preached about the Kingdom of God—the way life should be, the way life *would* be, when God's rule was established on earth—and he accepted into his entourage of disciples those persons that his society eschewed . . . women, tax collectors, and prostitutes . . .. And he hungout with, and helped, persons similarly cast-off by that same society . . . lepers, Samaritans, and Gentiles.

He scared the Roman authorities with his popularity and some of his counter cultural (even revolutionary) speech, and he confronted and alienated the Temple leadership on certain religious issues and theological topics. He was executed on a cross, a barbarous and cruel Roman method of capital punishment. Christian theology would later surmise and proclaim that he died to atone for the sins of the world.

But, he did not *stay* dead, and through a marvelous and miraculous act of God, he lives today. He *still* goes about doing good through his spirit, and you and I are *still* confronted by the claims of the Gospel and the promises of the Kingdom. And he *still* challenges us to care about other people and those who are helpless, powerless and oppressed as the "marginalized" of our world.

And yes, he *still* scares the powerful (when they holeup arrogantly in their personal kingdoms), the rich (when they clutch their wallets and purses and become calloused and indifferent to the needs of others), and the religiously smug (when they self-righteously become intolerant witch-hunters and downsize into spiritual pygmies). And yes, we *still* look to him as the source of our salvation, the source of our freedom from sin, and the source of the hope that our dreams, our visions and our very lives, will not suffer the extinction of death, but will amount to something and will make a difference!

You see, we Christians believe that this "Christmas stuff" is *true!* Our very worldview, and the actions we choose to pursue in the world, are predicated on the faith claim that *Christmas is not "humbug."* Imagine that! We Christians are bold to claim that a baby born in a feeding trough has changed and saved the world!

But it's true. It's not deception, it's not just glitter, it's not Christmas tinsel masquerading as "snow" on our Christmas trees in our homes! We affirm that it is the *truth:* "Jesus *is* the way, the truth and the life" (John 14:6a).

And, we point to this truth, we authenticate this "Good News" Gospel, we validate the Church and we legitimize the Christmas season, when our lives live out the following outrageous claims:

That God *loves* the world

That we ought to love our neighbors as well as ourselves

That mercy is healthier than revenge

That love lasts forever

That justice will prevail

That death is not the end

That money and materialism do not bring
the ultimate satisfaction

That hope is real and not merely
wishful thinking.

When we try to live this in our lives—

Not just one day a year
Not just one month a year
Not just one year of our lives

but *every* day, *every* month, *every* year, in *every* life—we demonstrate the **truth** of Christmas.

If every day was Christmas, how different life would be!
If not one day, but all the year, was lived in charity.
Had we the faith in miracles a child has Christmas morn,
Then love would be life's manger, and Christ would be
reborn.
Yet every day **is** *Christmas when we've truly learned to*
live—
That is, not how to get, but only how to give.

The Christmas story, the Christian tradition, the Christmas season, the Savior of the world on a bed of hay—

Is it a *hoax* or is it the **truth**?

Bah, humbug?

I am the way, the truth, and the life!

Rev. Clifford Chalmers Cain
Dean of the Chapel and Professor of Religion
Franklin College
Franklin

Clifford Chalmers Cain is a theologian, chapel dean, religion professor, scientist, photographer, former basketball player, traveler, trombonist, author, former college coach and father of two teenagers. The holder of a doctorate in theology and a doctorate in ecology, he received his formal education at Muskingum, Princeton, Leiden (The Netherlands), Vanderbilt, and Rikkyo (Tokyo). Ordained by the American Baptist Churches, USA, in 1975, Cliff served for twenty-one years as Dean of the Chapel and Professor of Philosophy and Religion at Franklin College in Franklin, Indiana. Currently, he is the occupant of an endowed chair as the Eli Lilly Professor of Religion at Berea College in Kentucky.

LISTENING TO OTHERS

In *Character Forged from Conflict: Staying Connected to God During Controversy*, Gary Preston writes:

> Back when the telegraph was the fastest means of long-distance communication, there was a story, perhaps apocryphal, about a young man who applied for a job as a Morse code operator. Answering an ad in the newspaper, he went to the address that was listed. When he arrived, he entered a large, noisy office. In the background a telegraph clacked away. A sign on the receptionist's counter instructed job applicants to fill out a form and wait until they were summoned to enter the inner office.
>
> The young man completed his form and sat down with seven other waiting applicants. After a few minutes, the young man stood up, crossed the room to the door of the inner office, and walked right in. Naturally the other applicants perked up, wondering what was going on. Why had this man been so bold? They muttered among themselves that they hadn't heard any summons yet. They took more than a little satisfaction in assuming the young man who went into

the office would be reprimanded for his presumption and summarily disqualified for the job.

Within a few minutes the young man emerged from the inner office escorted by the interviewer, who announced to the other applicants, "Gentlemen, thank you very much for coming, but the job has been filled by this young man."

The other applicants began grumbling to each other, and then one spoke up saying, "Wait a minute—I don't understand something. He was the last one to come in, and we never even got a chance to be interviewed. Yet he got the job. That's not fair."

The employer responded, "I'm sorry, but all the time you've been sitting here, the telegraph has been ticking out the following message in Morse code: If you understand this message, then come right in. The job is yours. None of you heard it or understood it. This young man did. So the job is his."

How many clear signals do we routinely miss? I've come to the conclusion that it is the unusual person who truly listens; most of us are too busy talking. Howard Clinebell, Jr. once wrote, "Many people are looking for an ear that will listen. They do not find it among Christians because Christians are talking when they should be listening."

I have to confess that listening carefully to others does not come naturally to me. I shudder when I recall the first counseling session I conducted as a young pastor. At age twenty-two and fresh out of college I was pastoring a small rural church when a young woman in the congregation called to ask if she could talk to me. Armed with the vast knowledge I had accumulated in my "Intro to Pastoral Counseling" course just completed, and a lot of enthusiasm, I welcomed this opportunity to be used of God.

What I had been taught by the college professor in my one counseling course could be boiled down to this simple maxim: "Shut up and listen." This I was prepared to do. I didn't do it. After this poor lady had shared a complicated story of difficult circumstances and business deals gone sour, I unconsciously shifted into "let's fix this" mode. Her tears only frustrated me as I prescribed some scripture that I was sure would help her see everything differently and suggested some action steps that I was sure would successfully lead her out of her difficulties.

I failed her miserably. As I reflect back on this incident with the benefit of 20/20 hindsight I understand that she wasn't coming for my help or advice. She simply needed someone who would listen to her, understand her and supportively pray for her.

In James 1:19 it says "My dear brothers, take note of this: Everyone should be quick to listen, slow to speak and slow to become angry." I sure wish I had been quicker to listen in that first counseling session and in hundreds of incidents since then. James is right on when he couples listening skills with being slow to speak and slow to be angry. When I'm speaking, I'm usually not listening. When I'm angry, I'm often not listening as well. When I'm not listening to others I am not helping them nor am I helping myself. Let me explain.

As a senior in college my world came crashing down around me. Carefully constructed plans I had laid out for my future fell apart. I was devastated. Full of grief and bewilderment I sought out a pastor friend whom I thought might be able to, in some way, help me with the oppressive heaviness I was feeling. I dropped by his home only to find that he was gone. His wife was a good friend also, so I risked sharing my pain with her. I probably made her uncomfortable by being so open and honest. It was obvious that she didn't really want to talk about what was going on in my life. "Things like that happen" was her observation before she changed the subject and moved on to more comfortably discussed matters. She was absolutely no help to me that day. I wonder how many times I have done that. When I'm not quick to listen I'm not helping others.

There is a powerful ministry in listening. In James 5:16 we are instructed to confess our sins to each other and to pray for each other so that we may be healed. When a brother or sister in Christ becomes open and honest about the needs in his or her life, there is a tremendous opportunity for spiritual, emotional and even physical healing to take place. What a privilege it is to hear the honest confessions of fellow Christians who want to be real in their relationships with God and man. What a healing influence we can have by listening, loving, accepting and prayerfully supporting those who have become so vulnerable.

Jan listened carefully as I preached from James 5:16, encouraging my congregation to be honest with one another. "Confessing our sins one to another can lead us to a place of healing" was the message that came across loud and clear. A few weeks later I heard Jan lament, "You sure have to be careful who you confess to. I learned that lesson in a hurry." Jan had opened up to a trusted friend. She had become vulnerable. She was betrayed. Instead of receiving healing she was the recipient of rejection and judgment. How incredibly sad!

For those of us with children it is so important for us to learn the ministry of listening. Some of us lament that our children no longer share openly with us. We miss the open communication of their early childhood days. What happened? Did they suddenly clam up, or have we faltered in listening well? I know that when I don't expect to be heard and accepted, I prefer to keep quiet.

What would happen if your child told you that he or she were gay? How would you respond to your brother who shared his struggle with an addiction to internet pornography? What if your pastor confided to you an alcohol problem in his life? We have difficulty processing these kinds of revelations. Something wells up within us that wants to cry out "That's not right!" The need of the moment, however, is not to make a value judgment. Those who vulnerably confess their struggles and their sins desperately need to be heard. How many of us have learned the art of listening well?

This is precisely why many people avoid the church like the plague. They have come to expect angry judgment and criticism from Christians who would rather tell them what's right and wrong, than labor with them as they seek to sort out their lives. They can be honest with the stranger next to them at the bar; it's safe to be real there. They cannot be honest with church people. When we aren't listening, we aren't helping others.

One of the most difficult tasks that ever was handed to me was the call asking me to inform my neighbors that their thirty-eight-year-old son had been killed in an automobile accident. "Sit down," I said as I entered their home. "I'm going to tell you the worst news you've ever heard." The tears flowed freely that afternoon. We sat there numbly trying to process the unthinkable.

After some time the phone rang. It was the daughter-in-law who had only hours earlier lost her husband. When my neighbor hung up the receiver after talking with her son's widow, she sighed and exclaimed, "I guess it really happened." Why did she say that? Did she not believe me when I shared the horrid news? Well, yes and no. While she understood that I was speaking the truth to her there was something inside of her that cried out "NO, THIS CAN'T BE!" We call it denial, which is a natural part of the grief process.

There are few of us who don't react to bad news with a hearty, "No!" Denial is a natural coping mechanism that is God-given. It buys us some time to gradually absorb the awfulness of news that we cannot fully absorb all at once. Denial can momentarily help us cope. When we get stuck in a state of denial, however, it is a terrible curse.

Aunt Katie was a strong woman who always seemed to be in control. Her life went wildly out of control a few years ago when her husband was diagnosed with cancer and within a few short weeks died. Aunt Katie lived nearly one-thousand miles away, but we made arrangements to stop by her home. She welcomed us into her home and prepared a nice meal. Dinner conversation was polite and cordial as we all ignored the "elephant in the room"—the fact that Uncle Frank had recently died.

I wanted to let her know that we were aware of her pain so I broached the subject. "It must be hard to go on without Uncle Frank; I'm sure you miss him very much," I offered. Aunt Katie couldn't handle that. She quickly rose from the table excused herself and retreated to her bedroom where we all knew she was sobbing. Several minutes passed when she returned to the table, her red eyes wiped dry. Quickly she offered another subject for discussion and we continued. I had touched a subject that she was not ready to talk about.

What have people been saying to you that you don't want to hear about? A good friend may have the courage to confront you with the problem you have with drinking, anger, gossip, an unhealthy relationship, or any one of a number of areas you'd rather not talk about. When I do not listen to friends or family members who care enough to confront me with the truth, I am the one who suffers. If I'm not listening, I'm not helping myself.

Often God will speak to us through the voice of someone

familiar, someone easily dismissed. As we resist listening to them, we often are resisting the very words of God. I can't help but think of King David who was confronted by the prophet Nathan. David was incensed as he heard Nathan tell the story about a rich man who had taken the pet lamb from a poor man who could afford no other. David's blood boiled as he readily recognized the injustice in the account being shared. Nathan looked David in the eye and explained that this story was really about him. "Thou art the man, King David." He had taken the wife of his own loyal army officer. This was a turning point in David's life, because he listened to words he would have rather not heard. As he listened he was led to repentance and forgiveness.

I have this vision for the church, which includes it being a safe place. It seems like if there's any place where I can be honest and real about the pain in my life it ought to be the church of Jesus Christ. My prayer is that the church would be a safe place where struggling people can be honest, be heard and not judged.

I also have a vision of the church being a place where we are ready to listen to the truth, even when it is painful. One of the marks of Christian maturity is learning to speak the truth in love. We've got plenty of churches that emphasize the truth, but lack in love. Others emphasize love at the expense of truth.

I want to make a commitment to seriously heed the exhortation found in James 1:19 where we are asked to "be quick to listen, slow to speak." I invite you to make this same commitment in your heart.

Rev. Doug Shoemaker
Westfield Friends Church
Westfield
January 9, 2000

Doug Shoemaker has served in Indiana Friends churches for over twenty-seven years. He graduated from Huntington College in 1978, receiving a Bachelor of Arts (BA) in Bible and Religion. In 1980 he received a Masters Degree from Huntington's Graduate School of Christian Ministries. He was recorded as a Friends minister that same year. He first served a twelve-year pastorate at the Hemlock Friends Church in Howard County. Since then he has served Westfield Friends Church in Hamilton County where he is in his thirteenth year. He and his wife, Kris, are the parents of three children, Kyle, Adam and Kelsie.

ACCEPTING PERSONAL RESPONSIBILITY

When the American surveillance plane had an emergency landing in China in April 2001, negotiations to free the twenty-four American detainees depended on the words used to say "I'm sorry." Now sorrow is defined as "a sense of loss or a sense of guilt or remorse." In most of the United States statements, our diplomats used the word regret, defined as "sorrow aroused by circumstances beyond one's control or power to repair." In the statement allowing the Americans to become free, the United States expressed its "sincere regret" and was "very sorry" for the loss of the Chinese pilot. A Chinese version of the letter said that President Bush was feeling *baoqian* (bow-chen), a colloquial word used to apologize for a relatively minor matter, such as being a bit late for an appointment. The Chinese wanted Bush to feel *daoqian* (dow-chen) which has a greater gravity to it, according to a Chinese language expert, Robert Ross.

But it's not only in diplomacy where we fail to find the right words and avoid accepting personal responsibility. A man in Netanya, Israel, was driving and using his cell phone, holding the wheel with the left hand while dialing with his right. He had a terrible auto accident. He claimed in court that he was not guilty.

Why? Because nowhere is it written in the law that driving is illegal while holding a cell phone with both hands! The judge found him guilty not only of bad driving but of *chutzpah*. What is the definition of *chutzpah*? It's exemplified by a person who kills both of his parents and then asks for the mercy of the court on the grounds that he is an orphan.

It seems that everybody wants to pass the buck. Stella Libeck spilled hot coffee in her lap, but it was McDonalds' fault. The Menendez brothers killed their parents, but it was the parents' fault. Brian Fortay didn't become a quarterback at the University of Miami, but it was the coach's fault. U.S. Olympic hockey player Jeremy Roenick, explaining why players' rooms were damaged, said, "We were sitting around playing cards and chairs would break underneath us." The parents of the Columbine gunman Dylan Klebold sued the Jefferson County Sheriff for negligence. U. S. House Majority Leader Dick Armey referred to his fellow congressman, Barney Frank, as Barney Fag. Armey said, "This is nothing more than an unintentional mispronunciation of another person's name that sounded like something it was not." From Tylenol capsules to Firestone tires, from personal injuries to murder, people have great difficulty in accepting responsibility for their actions.

A "Calvin and Hobbes" cartoon quotes Calvin: "Nothing I do is my fault. My family is dysfunctional and my parents won't empower me! Consequently, I'm not self-actualized! My behavior is addictive. Functioning in a disease process of toxic codependency! I need holistic healing and wellness before I'll accept any responsibility for my actions!" Hobbes responds, "One of us needs to stick his head in a bucket of ice water." Calvin says, "I love the culture of victimhood."

A few years ago attorney Alan Dershowitz wrote a book titled

The Abuse Excuse and Other Cop-Outs, Sob Stories, and Evasions of Responsibility. It almost sounds like the title for a book about Yom Kippur! He details reasons for crimes far more heinous than Eve eating the apple and passing the buck to the snake. Dershowitz enumerated forty excuses used either in court or by the media; each of these so-called defenses showed people abdicating personal responsibility, from the "chronic lateness syndrome" to "the minister made me do it," to "the Twinkie defense." Dershowitz notes that "at a deeper level, the excuse is a symptom of a general abdication of responsibility by individuals, families, groups and even nations. Its widespread acceptance is dangerous to the very tenets of democracy, which presupposes personal accountability for choices and actions."

Doesn't that sound like the meaning of this Day of Atonement? Our tradition is so open with our humanness. From the words of the rabbis of ancient days to the prayers we recite today, we acknowledge that we make mistakes, we err and we hurt feelings through our words or actions. And we do an intelligent thing about it as Jews. We spend this day acknowledging our stupid actions and our weaknesses, accepting them as part of life, hoping to repair relationships where there may be a breach, and striving always to become the children of God we were meant to be.

Rabbi Stephen Pearce suggests that we have become a nation of whiners, blamers and complainers, always pointing to someone else or external circumstances to explain our own shabby behavior. Looking around at all those who refuse to be accountable for their actions makes me wonder if humanity has made any real progress since the Garden of Eden. Perhaps because so many continue to fail to take responsibility for their own actions, we have not yet been able to return to Eden.

Whatever happened to personal responsibility? Fred Guy,

Director of the Hoffberger Center for Professional Ethics at the University of Baltimore, suggests that our consumer mentality has overwhelmed our moral and ethical priorities. Joseph Hough, Dean of the Divinity School at Vanderbilt, says we are obsessed with our self-interests. Bill Vitek, an Assistant Professor of Philosophy at Clarkson University, says that "our notions of personal responsibility are tied up in having a responsibility to something that is bigger then we are." So when we don't feel part of something larger like community, or society, or congregation, we lose the ties to others. "We jettison morality because we think happiness is more important." We've become standardless, says Robert Wertkin, a professor at the School of Social Work at Western Michigan University, "though we have to realize at some point people are going to have to take responsibility for themselves."

Is this any different from our teachings about Pharaoh, who hardened his heart and began to feel that responsibility was beyond his control? Pharaoh could have given up his stubbornness and fewer plagues would have landed on Egypt. But his ego, his power, his concern for authority got in the way. Judaism teaches that we all have free will, that we can act according to our good inclination, *yetzer hatov,* or our evil inclination, *yetzer hara.* In the beginning, the evil inclination is like a spider web—it is easy to step out of its grasp. But later it becomes like a heavy rope, which burdens us and leaves us bound by ill will.

Accepting personal responsibility, always seen as a private matter, has become a growing tradition at the corporate level as well. Public contrition, when handled immediately and well, is completely understood by the consumer. In 1987 Toshiba publicly apologized for secretly selling submarine equipment to the USSR. In 1994 Intel apologized for faulty computer chips. Coors ran full page ads under the headline "We goofed" after selling a bad batch of beer. Tylenol apologized when poisoning occurred, removed all its products off the shelf, repackaged, repented and came back strong. McDonalds took out full page ads recently when prize money was embezzled.

Yet there isn't an American citizen who felt comfortable with Bill Clinton's so-called apologies, Gary Condit's stonewalling, the national accounting firms' weak explanation for corporate frauds they certified or the humble pie eaten by corporations when they do wrong. It takes courage to admit the wrong, to take responsibility for it, to express our regret, fix it and to provide honest assurance that it won't happen again. And when we do our part—to acknowledge our wrong, make a meaningful apology, make restitution and take concrete steps to make sure that this won't happen again, we are entitled to decent treatment in return. As we have a right to expect forgiveness from others, we also have to give it to ourselves.

The poet D.H. Lawrence wrote:

I am not a mechanism, an assembly of various sections.
And it is not because the mechanism is working wrongly, that
I am ill.

I am ill because of wounds to the soul, to the deep emotional self
and the wounds to the soul take a long, long time,
only time can help
and patience, and a certain difficult repentance
long difficult repentance, realization of life's mistake,
and the freeing oneself
from the endless repetition of the mistake
which mankind at large has chosen to sanctify.

An anonymous author wrote:

On this Day of Atonement we will seek not to escape

responsibility for our own selves. We will not fault parents, siblings or childhood traumas for the weaknesses we display. Nor will we blame society, the economy, or our institutions for their failure to make us perfect. Judaism teaches us that we are free, not free to do anything we want, for we have obligations to others, nor free to be anyone we wish, for we are influenced by others.

We are free to choose, a dozen times a day how we shall react to life's challenges, and in this small way to mold ourselves to become better than we are. On this Day of Atonement we need to accept responsibility for our own selves. We cannot be perfect, continuously happy and successful, always attractive, popular and healthy. We seek only to be better, to be a little kinder, braver, and more patient. To share a few more simchas, *to do a few more* mitzvot, *be at one with ourselves, our values and our dreams, as well as being at one with our people, our tradition and our God.*

How do we return? We follow the words of Isaiah, from tomorrow's *Haftarah*, our prophetic reading. The prophet challenges us to remember why we fast, feel uncomfortable and afflict our souls. It's not just to make us feel hungry, thirsty or tired, but to teach us a lesson, "To loose the fetters of wickedness, to undo the bonds of the yoke and to let the oppressed go free." It's our responsibility to clothe the naked, feed the hungry and shelter the homeless.

Rabbi Vernon Kurtz adds, "It should awaken our very souls to what is happening around us. Isaiah's words remind us of our responsibilities to others. We cannot and we must not find excuses to abdicate our responsibilities. Instead, we must assume the obligations that are inherent in our lives and work toward accomplishing our tasks."

Many of you know that I am a mediocre golfer. But I always

admired the class and dignity with which Payne Stewart lived his life. Rich, handsome, successful, a multi-millionaire, he was one of golf's most recognizable figures because of his knickers. Stewart had a serious problem off the course; he once went on TV and did a tasteless imitation of a Chinese person. Later, he apologized for what he had done and said he was sorry. Stewart wanted to get better at handling the public and went to a media seminar. It didn't work overnight, but he continued to work and change. "It took me a while to get it through my thick head that I wasn't the only person trying to do a job. I wasn't doing that. I know I'm not perfect. I still make mistakes, but I'm trying. I really am trying."

In 1998 Payne Stewart led the U. S. Open by four shots with one round to play. Lee Jantzen beat him by a stroke. Once, Stewart would have stalked away after such a defeat and been snappish and rude to reporters. But this time was different. He was gracious, patient, kept his sense of humor and showed the reporters respect they didn't know he had. The next year he won the U. S. Open by dropping a fifteen-foot putt on the final hole. In the Ryder Cup in 1999 his match with Colin Montgomerie was the last one to be decided, since the United States had already clinched the cup. Montgomerie had a twenty-foot putt to win the match. If he missed, the match would be a draw. Stewart walked over, picked the ball up and handed it to him. He gave him the putt and the win. Later, Stewart said, "It didn't matter one bit to me if I won my match, as long as my team won. It was the right thing to do."

Stewart didn't always get things right, but he never once claimed he was never wrong. He accepted responsibility for his actions, didn't pass the buck, admitted his mistakes, learned from them and kept on growing. May his model be an example for us all.

Amen.

Rabbi Morley T. Feinstein
Temple Beth-El
South Bend
On the observance of Yom Kippur

Rabbi Morley Feinstein is the new Senior Rabbi of University Synagogue, Los Angeles. For the past fifteen years he was Senior Rabbi Temple Beth-El in South Bend. He graduated from U.C. Berkeley, Phi Beta Kappa with Highest Honors. From 1981-1984, following ordination at the Hebrew Union College of Jewish Institute of Religion, he served Temple Beth-El in San Antonio, Texas. Rabbi Feinstein has published a book, *The Jewish Law Review*, as well as numerous articles in publications such as *The Jewish Spectator, Journal of Reform Judaism* and *Midstream*. He has been a NPR commentator for the South Bend local affiliate WVPE. He is one of the contributors to the prayerbook, the *Gates of Prayer For Shabbat and Weekdays*.

GOD LOVES YOU

Mark 1:29-38.

Simon Peter and his companions searched for Jesus early in the morning.

They found Him in a deserted place—praying. "Everybody's looking for you," they said. They were so impressed by His miracles that they thought He would want to rejoin the crowds and continue working miracles.

I think they must have been a little surprised at our Lord's response: "Let us go to the nearby villages that I may preach there also." He was teaching them in no uncertain terms that His mission was primarily preaching. Everything else, even the miracles, was part of that mission of preaching.

What was the message He came to preach?

"God loves you." It was that simple.

Remember the night when Nicodemus came secretly to talk with Jesus? In the course of their conversation, our Lord put it very clearly, "God loved the world so much that He gave up His only begotten Son, so that those who believe in Him may not perish, but have eternal life."

Our Lord repeated that message in many ways during his life. And at the Last Supper, to make sure the Apostles understood, He expressed it in a number of ways, especially in those beautiful words: "As the Father loves Me (infinitely), so I love you (infinitely)."

Jesus preached the message of God's love for us in words. But He also demonstrated it in loving actions. "He went about doing good."

Take the wedding feast at Cana, for example. As Br. Giles will tell you, the first thing you do when you're planning a party is to make sure you have plenty of food and drink. This poor couple were either too poor to provide enough wine—or they underestimated their friends' thirst. Our Lord saw their embarrassment, so He created "instant wine" to relieve that embarrassment. That's God's love in action.

Or think of the widow of Nain. She was on the way to the cemetery to bury her only son, her provider. She was heartbroken, not only because she had lost her son, but also because she was worried about how she could provide for herself without him. Jesus sensed her misery. So He restored her son to life. That's God's love in action.

Another example: Lazarus. Our Lord felt sorry for Mary and Martha over the loss of their brother, Lazarus. But He also felt the loss of Lazarus personally. As the Gospel tells us, "Jesus wept. 'See how he loved him,' the Jews said." So Jesus brought Lazarus back to life. That's God's love in action.

One more example: The cure of Peter's mother-in-law in today's gospel reading. This may be stretching the point a bit, but I've often wondered why St. Mark adds the comment: "The fever left her and she waited on them."

Could it be that one of the motives for the miracle was that the apostles were hungry and Peter's mother-in-law was the only cook in the house? Whatever our Jesus' motivation may have been, this was one more evidence of God's love in action.

I've often thought you could go all through the gospels and find one miracle after another demonstrating God's love in action. And not only miracles. Jesus preached God's love in action by everything He said. For me, one of the most powerful examples is His Love for children.

St. Mark describes it so vividly: "They brought children to Him, asking him to touch them. The disciples rebuked those who brought them. But Jesus was indignant at seeing this. 'Let the children come to me,' He said. 'Do not keep them back' . . . and He embraced them, laid His hands upon them and blessed them."

Isn't that a magnificent scene? The Son of God, the busiest man who ever lived, takes time out to express His love for little children. The part that really thrills me is that last sentence: "He embraced them, laid His hands upon them and blessed them." That's showing God's love in action. And the greatest thing about it is: *we* are those children.

That leads to the ultimate expression of God's love for us: our Lord's death on the cross. He said, " No one has greater love than this . . . to give up his life for his friends." That was certainly Christ's way of showing God's love in action.

Abbey Press used to have a small scroll that said it well:

I asked Jesus, "how much do you love me?" "This much,"
He said, and stretched out His arms and died.

How does all this make you feel? It ought to send us in orbit, make us very happy. Here's how the Curé of Ars put it: "If we only knew how much God loves us, we would die from joy!"

One day he said the same thing in a little different way: "It's always springtime in a heart that loves God."

Two final notes: Julian of Norwich, the 14th century mystic, said:

> *The greatest honor you can give Almighty God— greater than all your sacrifices and mortifications—is to live joyfully because of the knowledge of God's love.*

Psalms 30 summarizes it perfectly:

Lord, let me be glad and rejoice in your love.

Fr. Eric Lies
St. Meinrad Archabbey
St. Meinrad
February 6, 2000, 5th Sunday

Fr. Eric Lies, OSB, is a monk of Saint Meinrad Archabbey, St. Meinrad, Indiana. A native of Aurora, Illinois, he attended Saint Meinrad Seminary and was ordained in 1945. After teaching in the Seminary for ten years, he became manager of Abbey Press. In 1968, he joined the Development staff, where he worked until July 1, 1994.

During his fifty-seven years as a priest, Fr. Eric has given many retreats, mostly weekend retreats for lay men and women. He is perhaps best known as a calligrapher, and his entries in the Indiana State Fair have won a number of awards.

Raising Children
with Strong Faith

One of the most precious gifts that God has given us is the gift of our children. Like other valuable gifts, this gift also has to be cherished, protected and preserved. I and my wife of nearly thirty years have been blessed with four such gifts and we have tried our best to raise them as children of faith. In a society where sometimes secular schools and media trivialize religion, it is not easy these days for parents to raise children with a strong faith.

Many of us, even grown-ups, sometimes have difficulty in identifying with faith, but not my children. My eldest daughter who is now married and gave me my first grandchild, always wore *hijab* (head cover) from middle school to college years and never dated. My eldest son, when he entered high school, noted that the restrooms for boys had no doors, thus no privacy. He walked straight to the principal's office and said, "I am a Muslim and I need privacy, therefore, at least one restroom should have a door." The principal was so impressed with his modesty that he ordered doors for each of the restrooms. My second son, when he was in middle school, was in the cafeteria line and bought some snacks. The cashier gave him more change by mistake than he deserved. He immediately returned the extra change to her. The cashier was impressed and said, "You are a good Muslim." My fourteen-year-old daughter's best friends are not only Muslim, but Christian and Jewish girls as well. I am proud of all of my children, as any parent of faith should be.

Children can be moulded. Whatever falls on them leaves a permanent impression. Therefore, we should be careful what falls on them to become that impression. If we become what we want our children to become, they may become what we want them to. The parents who let their children grow without faith get a "wake up call" when their kids are in trouble in the teenage years. Sometimes I get phone calls from parents saying they need a Muslim counselor, but I am not a counselor, I am a physician. Calls involve such requests as "my daughter is in trouble" or "we found out my son is on drugs." Such unfortunate things are happening to our children irrespective of the faith they are born into. Parents must teach faith by examples they set rather than by lectures of morality they give.

Our children are not perfect but neither are we adults. There has always been a generation gap and parents have complained about their children. In 400 BC Socrates wrote, "Children now love luxury. They show disrespect for their elders. They are monsters and not obedient. Children in the house contradict their parents, chatter unnecessarily, gobble up their food at the table, cross their legs and terrorize their teachers." However, what could be considered disrespectful behavior by children in school in the 1940s, such as talking during class, chewing gum, running in the hallway, wearing improper clothing or not putting paper in the wastepaper basket, has now been replaced by drug abuse, alcohol abuse, suicide, pregnancy, rape, robbery, assault, burglary, arson, carrying guns to school and killing fellow students and teachers. We leave our children in this society under these circumstances in schools and expect them to grow as children with faith without our help.

We must recognize the pressures that our children are exposed to. According to statistics available, the average drinking age starts at age twelve. By the senior year in high school, one out of every twenty students has been drinking alcohol regularly. Nearly half of the teens who have committed suicide were intoxicated at the time. Nearly every teen who was involved in an auto accident as a passenger, had a teenage driver who was intoxicated with alcohol. Ninety-three percent of children in grades for and five consider cocaine as a drug but only twenty-one percent of the same say alcohol is a drug too. In our society, 2,000 children are physically abused each day, over 3,000 children run away from home, and around the same number see their parents being divorced every day. Some 2,000 pre-teen girls become pregnant every day. A child watching television only two to three hours per day watches about 9,000 violent scenes and around 3,500 sexually suggestive scenes every year. We parents have different set of rules for ourselves and our children. Why is it that drinking alcohol after age twenty-one is OK but not before twenty-one? Does the liver get better after age twenty-one? We must set examples for our children for the rules that we want them to follow.

A certain woman took her son to Prophet Mohammad and requested him to tell the child not to eat too many sweets because she was afraid sweets would ruin his health and his teeth. The Prophet asked her to bring him back after one week and she did. Then he told the child about the dangers of taking too many sweets and the boy understood and made a promise not to eat them. The companions of the Prophet asked, after the mother and child left, why did he wait one week to tell the child. He said, "I wanted to practice giving up sweets myself first."

Now, before we tell our youth to give up television for a week, can we first practice the same for ourselves? Many parents buy their children expensive clothes, shoes, toys and other gifts. However, the best gift is the gift of good manners. Prophet Mohammad has said, "a father (or mother) teaching his child good manners is better than giving a bushel of grain in charity." We parents have no control over who our children socialize with in school, but we can find a better social outlet for them after school hours. That is why it is so important for communities of faith to organize programs for youth of their own. Muslim youth of North America, a national organization with a chapter in every major city, now has brought Muslim youth together, not only to learn about faith but to socialize with each other in permissible settings to include camping, debates and sports activities.

It may not be possible in this day and age to get rid of television from every home, but we can help children select programs that are conducive to their growth in faith. We should watch those programs with them, if possible. In the same context, the Internet is a double-edged sword. While it is a tool of learning and information for our children, sometimes it can give wrong messages or lure our children with sexually oriented material. Every family must use certain parental controls over what the children can or can not watch. One recommendation is to have the computer in a common place where the child would hesitate to watch such programs offered by the wrong websites. It is not enough just to tell the youth that they shouldn't do this and that but we must give reasoning about right and wrong from the faith prospective. We must teach them the values from their faith, whether it is Christianity, Judaism or Islam so that they start thinking why they should behave differently than those without faith-based values.

Faith empowers children with their rights. They have a right to learn and practice their faith even if one of their parents is not practicing religion. They have a right to receive love, discipline and care from their parents but they must give the parents the same rights as well. Parents have a right to know about their children and the factors which influence them. The rights of God are above the rights of parents and children. God, who created us, has a right to be worshiped, to be believed in and to have His injunctions followed. Muslim children are told in Quran, (17: 23-24).

> *Your Lord has commanded that you worship no one but Him and be kind to your parents. If either or both of them reach old age, do not say a word of contempt nor repulse them but speak to them with kindness and honor and lower to them your wings of submission and say, "My Lord have mercy on them as they cared for me when I was an infant."*

If both parents and children submit to the will of God, there will be love and peace in the family. We must teach our children the value of life and hatred for violence. From the very beginning, they should be taught to respect others who look different from them. They must also be taught to control their anger when provoked and to remain calm and cool. Access to the tools of expression of anger should be discouraged whether it is guns or any other weapons at the same level as use of drugs and alcohol. We should help our children grow in peace and love and in faith, not only in God, but also in themselves and their country.

Shahid Athar, MD
Al-Fajr Mosque
Indianapolis
A Friday sermon

In addition to being a practicing physician, Dr. Athar is an Islamic writer and speaker, having authored over one hundred articles and five books on Islamic topics, which can be read on line at www.islam-usa.com. He has been giving Friday sermon at the mosques in Indianapolis for the last twenty years. He is founder/President of the Islamic Society of Greater Indianapolis (ISGI) and Interfaith Alliance of Indiana (IAI). He can be reached via e-mail: sathar3624@aol.com.

TRAVELING IN FAR AND STRANGE LANDS

Matthew 2:13 (NIV)

Thirty years before the cross was considered as a method to kill Jesus, He had to flee for His life.

You see there was something about the birth of our Lord and the surrounding circumstances which frightened King Herod. The wise men were the final blow to his aroused jealousies. He tried to use them to discover the whereabouts of the infant Jesus, born in Bethlehem. He asked them to return to his palace as soon as they had seen the child and presented their gifts. The wise men were warned in a dream not to return to the envious king. They didn't and the old tyrant was furious. He flew into an infantile rage. He would fix this Jewish baby boy who was receiving so much fanfare! He ordered the death of all male children under two years of age in the Bethlehem area.

From the very first days, Jesus' life was not an easy one. A new life had entered the earthly realm. It was not just any combination of flesh and blood. The Son of God was born to Joseph and Mary. Had He been less promising His problem of existence would have been greatly lessened.

Joseph, Mary and Jesus made their way to Egypt, a far and strange land. Their journey was not a long one by our standards. We have no way of knowing the exact route the family followed. The shortest distance between Bethlehem and the borders of Judea to the south was approximately thirty miles. It is safe to say they traveled, at least, one hundred miles to Egypt. In our automobiles this takes about two hours. It took Jesus and His parents days and perhaps weeks. Walking by foot or even riding a donkey over treacherous terrain can be very time-consuming. Joseph was a good man and tried to do what God commanded. God told him to take the child to Egypt for His safety. Joseph was a poor carpenter and must have wondered how he would finance such a trip. Nevertheless, he didn't argue the matter. Father, mother and their bundle of joy set out for Egypt, a country both remote and unfamiliar.

A portion of Matthew 2:13 (NIV) reads: ". . . an angel of the Lord appeared to Joseph in a dream. 'Get up,' he said, 'take the child and his mother and escape to Egypt. Stay there until I tell you, for Herod is going to search for the child to kill him.'" Joseph was already fond of Jesus and was anxious about His safety. He took the child to Egypt, a far and strange land.

If we will, you and I can make a splendid and instructive similarity at this point. Does not our Father take us into far and strange lands? Does He not do so that we might avoid spiritual stagnation and even death? We do not relish or willingly accept tragedy, pain, sorrow or failure. Nevertheless, they have their place. On bended knee you and I are summoned to admit the truth of the matter.

We do not like the blistering hot sun, desolate ravines, and scrubby trees in the *Land of Tragedy.*

Much too often we react in bitterness.

A sword is gouged into our soft religious flesh, and it hurts.

An automobile accident has taken the lives of two dear friends. They were good, likable people. But we had never given them a *serious* invitation to worship with us on a specific Sunday morning. Oh, we hinted a few times that their lives might be greatly helped by worshipping with us and others. Our words betrayed us. They were interpreted to mean the Church is something less than the Body of Christ and a spiritual Fellowship of Believers. Every time we visualize the crinkled hood, smashed sides and broken windows of their automobile, the pen of bitterness writes another negative impression.

Red-hot coals touch a tongue not yet fully dedicated to Christ. A seminary professor and outstanding preacher once told us without warning, "I don't like God." Some of us stared in amazement at what we heard. One or two very conservative chaps were ready to register a complaint with the Dean. Some were thinking along the lines of psychiatric help for our teaching brother. Well, several minutes later in the class period he said, "I don't like God because several years ago He took away our baby's life that I wanted more than my own." God spoke to him in the only way he would listen. The professor's point was made and the softness in his face told us the story of tragedy remade into triumph. There is no absolute law that says you and I have to react in bitterness to such experiences.

We can respond in love to the God who is an expert in healing broken hearts.

Our trouble is in trying to use our own strength in mending our brains and soothing our emotions. We take a little sweetness and patch it on a place worn raw by our internal turmoil. We produce a mask of kind understanding and wear it on suitable occasions. We lift our heads far higher than they should be for proper posture and pretend our injuries don't show. We talk ourselves into becoming interested in some new fad in hopes it will make us forget.

We can save a lot of time and energy by going directly to God. A great deal of shoe leather can be saved simply by falling upon our knees. Many sentences can be saved simply by articulating with sincerity the words, "God help me!"

God is Master of creating. Ah, but He is also Master of re-creating!

The *Land of Tragedy* may or may not be a manifestation of God's wrath. It is a means to quicken and perfect our religious lives. Another far and strange land beckons to us to share its rewards.

We do not like the gigantic thistles, sharp rocks and parched earth in the *Land of Pain*.

We are all too ready to wallow in self-pity.

A leg is badly broken, and hospitalization for many days is the result. We admit it isn't the first leg which has ever been broken. The room accommodations are good. One nurse likes to give orders, but the others are quite understanding. The doctor seems to be doing his best. We try the "stiff-upper-lip" routine, but it is only an awkward mechanism. We were sent to our bed of affliction to take inventory of our lives, but we can only feel the pain of the body which is intense. We wouldn't take time to think about God, but He makes us stop long enough for us to know that He is still God and will continue to be forever.

A son has gone off to the army. The mental anguish keeps our brains throbbing. Will he have enough to eat? He will, and all six courses will probably be heaped in one delicious, delectable pile. Will someone wash his clothes? Yes, he will—at least for several weeks. Will he have his shoes polished? He had better have. Our son is gone and God knows what he needs. Our Father also knows the degree to which we have done our work as mother and father. If we have not done an acceptable job of rearing him, we should not pity ourselves. We should pity the top sergeant, the commanding officer, or—better still—our son.

Self-pity is a terrible waste of time.

There are always others who are experiencing greater pain.

Let's view together three brief word-pictures. A young man being brutally attacked by a malignant tumor. An old lady with both legs pinned beneath her dying husband's automobile. A man at the peak of his career stricken by spinal meningitis.

There is always somebody who is in greater pain than we are. We complain of our poor hearing, until we notice a deaf mute. We complain of our poor eyesight, until we see a blind beggar.

The *Land of Pain* is not welcomed. It is a method to shake us out of step with the deathmarch of souls. Another land in the distance calls us.

We do not like the hail-stones, thunderclaps and lightning flashes experienced in the *Land of Sorrow*. The easy way out is to respond in sulkiness.

A life-long partner in business absconds with all available funds. You are financially ruined. You want to tear everything in sight to pieces. The business is gone for all practical purposes, but that isn't the most important event. One that you trusted over the years has shown complete disloyalty. He has hurt you deeply and the temptation to withdraw from life in resentment and apply his betrayal to all other human beings has begun to get the upper hand.

Years ago you loved a young man and wanted to marry him. With great pride you introduced him to a girlfriend. They fell in love and were married. As the years have passed, you have remained single and the resentment increases with each passing day. Your abilities have lain dormant so long you can feel them slipping away forever. You have become a "psychological cripple."

There is no purpose in inflicting such destructive punishment.

Sorrow can be used to push us into losing ourselves in worthwhile activities.

If some sorrow is weighing us down, we should not ask that it be lifted. We should appeal to our God to put us to work in those areas where He needs us. If we can't find adventures that really count, it is safe to say we have never earnestly asked. Our prayers were timid requests which expected little or nothing. Beneficial activities cannot completely blot out sorrow which is deep-seated, and this is to our advantage. Becoming engrossed in such activities is not a running away from reality. It is running to our God!

Our parents and grandparents' admonition was, "Don't cry over spilled milk." There is a wisdom in that injunction. However, we need to add the words, "but don't sit around and let the cup remain empty." Even the most expensive and potentially useful vessel is subject to deterioration.

The *Land of Sorrow* is intended to lift us above and beyond ourselves. A final far and strange land awaits us.

We don't like the torrential rain, pesky sleet, and heavy snow in the *Land of Failure*.

Failing to attain a worthy goal is often met by "sour grapes." We become scornful of the thing we are after only because we cannot have it or did not get it.

There was an opening on the varsity basketball team. A lad on the second team could see himself in a varsity suit. He would capture that unfilled position! He worked very hard at the next practices, and the coach was impressed. He did everything within his power to gain that coveted position. The coach picked someone else. Upon leaving the gym he told himself, "Oh, well it wasn't worth having anyway."

This isn't purely a teenage characteristic, is it? Adults use the same mechanism. Some of us probably react so often this way we aren't even aware of it.

There was an opening in the store chain, but we weren't selected. Our reply, "It wasn't worth the additional responsibility." Isn't that interesting?

There was a retired farmer seeking a good tenant, but we didn't make the grade. Our reply, "It wasn't the type of farm land desired anyway." Again, isn't it interesting?

Whether they be big or little failures, "sour grapes" is not the solution.

Those who are successful have learned one small, highly significant lesson: profit from your mistakes. The most successful people in the world have failed dismally in one or several things.

The lives of the saints are sprinkled by this common occurrence. Do we recall what their secret was? They sought out the reasons for their inadequacies and called upon God to supply the essentials for victorious living. We can do no more than that today, but we *can do* that.

A bit of caution: We ought to be sure we have actually failed and have not simply been termed a failure by someone's irresponsible indictment.

The Apostle Peter failed three times in a few hours. Had this not happened, we may never have known him! Perhaps in God's grand design it had to happen in order for his greatness to emerge.

Thus, we have briefly traversed the *Land of Failure.*

"Taking what life hands out and doing something with it" is not an eloquent expression. Not all truths need to be stated with eloquence. May God continually remind us.

Christians are called upon to see the *unusual opportunity* in *the unpromising situation.* This is the difference between anemic and dynamic Christianity. Such a difference is colossal and points to whether or not "dem dead bones gonna rise again."

Our Father does take us into far and strange lands to refresh and reactivate our inner lives. Then—if we will—we can be those radiant, outgoing Christians. Then, internally and externally, we can testify to the riches of Jesus Christ.

Rev. Donald Charles Lacy
Yorktown United Methodist Church
Yorktown
March 3, 2002

Dr. Lacy has served United Methodist churches across the state of Indiana for well over forty years. He received the BS (1945) and MA (1958) degrees from Ball State University and taught Social Studies and English in Jay County. Christian Theological Seminary granted him the M.Div. (1961) and D.Min. (1976) degrees. In addition to his pastoral ministry, he is also widely known as an author and an ecumenist. He is a native of Henry and Delaware Counties.

Remember That You Are Dust and to Dust You Shall Return

These words are spoken every Ash Wednesday as we receive the ashes on our foreheads. These words are spoken every Ash Wednesday in order to remind us of a fact that we try hard to forget: we are all going to die. Intellectually we all know we're going to die, but have we emotionally and spiritually accepted this fact?

Five years ago I made available to my congregation a "Funeral Planning Guide." It asks questions such as: "Do you wish to be cremated, buried, or placed in a mausoleum? Where do you want your remains placed? What scriptures do you want read at your funeral? What hymns would you like sung?" Three years ago we offered a "Death and Dying" class in our church, revised the "Funeral Planning Guide," and offered it to the congregation again. And last year I once more made the guides available. After five years of making the "Funeral Planning Guide" available to my congregation, only three have been filled out and returned to me. I wonder how many people here, who are in reasonably good health, have made out a will? I would guess many have not.

Remember that you are dust and to dust you shall return.

Why are we so frightened by death and try to deny it? First of all, I suppose we fear old age and the deterioration of our bodies.

We fear our organs slowly wearing out and our muscles weakening. We fear all the aches and pains, the daily medications, and no longer getting a good night's sleep because of all the discomfort and having to go to the bathroom repeatedly.

We fear losing all the things we have slowly accumulated throughout our lives that fill our homes. We fear the day when we will need to move into a tiny apartment because we can no longer maintain a home, and we have to get rid of many of our belongings. And perhaps a few years later we will have to move into a small room in a nursing home, and all we possess will need to go into four drawers of a dresser.

We fear gradually losing each of our friends and family members until we are all alone.

We fear the moment of death itself—not being able to breathe. Will we feel like we're suffocating? Will we feel our heart stop beating? When I was about ten years old I remember being afraid of death and asking God, "Please let me die quietly in my sleep." I didn't want to know it was happening. Sometimes death comes this way, but statistically that isn't how it usually happens.

We fear the possibility that after death there is nothing, that death is oblivion.

And we fear that we will be forgotten. When I go into antique shops I often see old photographs from a hundred years ago. I do not know who the people are in the photographs, and neither do the people running the antique shop. And then it occurs to me that I have two drawers at home that are chock full of photographs. But after I die, most of them will be thrown out or lost, and eventually the few that remain will come into the hands of people who will not know who the people are in the photographs.

Remember that you are dust and to dust you shall return.

Woody Allen once said, "I don't want to achieve immortality through my work; I want to achieve immortality through not dying." We don't have that option, and so we human beings try to be important while we're alive, or try to be wealthy and as comfortable as possible, or try to make our mark on the world so we won't be forgotten. But all of these pursuits are an artificial immortality. They all die with us or soon thereafter. The great lesson of life is this: to accept our mortality and trust in God.

There is an ancient Jewish legend about how Moses died. You'll remember that Moses lived to be one hundred and twenty years old, but he was not allowed to cross over into the Promised Land with the Israelites. Instead, he could only see the Promised Land from the top of Mount Nebo. The story goes like this:

When God saw that Moses was ready to die, he said to the angel Gabriel, "Go fetch me the soul of Moses!" But Gabriel said, "How can I approach and take the soul of one who has done so many miracles? O Lord of the world, Adam sinned against you, and therefore you removed your glory from him and bestowed it upon Moses whom you love."

God answered, "But even Noah, who found favor in my eyes because of his righteousness, died." Gabriel said, "Noah saved only himself and his family when you sent a flood upon the world. Nor did he care to pray to you for the lives of the people who were destroyed. But Moses would not leave your presence until you had promised him that you would forgive the people their sin."

God answered, "But even Abraham, who was kind and righteous, did not escape death." Gabriel said, "Abraham was indeed a great man, for he gave food to the poor and provided them with all their wants, but this was done by him in a settled land, whereas Moses provided an entire nation with food in the wilderness."

God answered, "No mortal may escape death! Such is my decree!" Then Gabriel went on to plead, "O Lord of the world, please give this mission to someone besides me!"

God then turned to the angel Michael and said to him, "Go and fetch me the soul of Moses!" But Michael answered, "How can I presume to approach and take the soul of him who is equal in your eyes to sixty myriads of people?"

So God turned to the Angel of Death and said to him, "Go and fetch me the soul of Moses!" The Angel of Death was happy to do this since this was his usual job. He took his sword and wrapped himself in wrath and hastened to Moses. But when he saw the face of Moses and gazed into his eyes, the radiance of which was equal to that of the sun, he trembled and drew back.

Moses said to him, "What is it you want of me?" The Angel of Death replied, "The God of heaven and earth, who created all souls, has sent me to take your soul." "I will not give you my soul!" cried Moses. "Leave me at once for I stand here declaring the glory of God!" To which the Angel of Death replied, "The heavens declare the glory of God and the firmament shows his handiwork." But Moses said, "I will silence the heavens and the firmament, and I myself will narrate his glory."

The Angel of Death then said, "All souls since the creation of the world were delivered into my hands. Now let me approach you and take your soul too." "Go away!" cried Moses. "I will not give you my soul!"

In great terror the Angel of Death returned to God and said, "Lord of the world, I am unable to approach the man to whom you sent me." God's wrath was now kindled and he said, "Go to him again and fetch me his soul!"

So the Angel of Death drew his sword from its sheath, girded himself in cruelty, and in a towering fury went off to see Moses. When Moses saw the Angel of Death, he arose in anger and took his staff which had parted the sea and which is inscribed with the

Ineffable Name, and struck the Angel of Death, blinding him.

At that moment a voice from heaven called out, "Moses, your last second is at hand!" Hearing this, Moses prayed, "Lord of the world, be gracious and merciful to me. Do not surrender my soul into the hands of the Angel of Death!" Then the heavenly voice spoke once again, "Be comforted Moses. I myself will take your soul. I myself will bury you."

God revealed himself from the highest heaven, and the angels Gabriel and Michael stood on either side of Moses as Moses lay down. And the Lord said to Moses, "Shut your eyes." Moses obeyed. Then the Lord said, "Press your hand upon your heart." Moses did so. Then the Lord said, "Place your feet in order." Moses obeyed God's command.

Then the Lord addressed the soul of Moses, "My daughter! For one hundred and twenty years you have inhabited this undefiled body of dust. But now your hour has come. Rise and fly into Paradise!" But the soul replied, "I know that you are the God of spirits and of souls. You created me and put me into the body of this righteous man. Is there anywhere in the world a body so pure and holy as this one? During these one hundred and twenty years I have learned to love it, and now I do not wish to leave it."

God replied, "My daughter, do not hesitate, but come forth for your end has come. I will place you in the highest heaven and let you dwell, like the Cherubim and the Seraphim, beneath the throne of Divine Majesty." But the soul replied, "Lord of the world! I desire to remain with this righteous man, for he is purer and holier than the very angels. When the angels descended from heaven to earth they became corrupt, but this creature of flesh and blood has not sinned from the moment he saw the light of day. Let me therefore, I implore you, remain where I am."

Then God bent over the face of Moses and kissed him. At

once the soul leaped up in joy and with the kiss of God flew into Paradise.[1]

Lent begins tonight. The season of Lent is the story of death—specifically, Jesus' death. For six and a half weeks we will follow Jesus to his death. The season of Lent will pose two questions for us: First, will Jesus try to avoid death? Will he use his God-given power to protect himself and become immortal, never having to die? And the second question is this: Will we follow Jesus and trust him all the way to our own cross?

Remember that you are dust and to dust you shall return.

These are not words of despair; these are the words that lead to life. Accept your humanness, accept your mortality, trust in God, and death becomes a doorway to God. As the "Prayer of Saint Francis" says:

> *For it is in giving that we receive, it is in pardoning that we are pardoned, and in dying that we are born to eternal life.*

When we follow Jesus all the way to the cross, we will experience what Paul experienced when he said:

> *What then are we to say about these things? If God is for us, who is against us? He who did not withhold his own Son, but gave him up for all of us, will he not with him also give us everything else? Who will bring any charge against God's elect? It is God who justifies. Who is to condemn? It is Christ Jesus who died, yes, who was raised, who is at the right hand of God, who indeed intercedes for us. Who will separate us from the love of Christ? Will hardship or distress,*

or persecution, or famine, or nakedness, or peril, or sword?
No, in all these things we are more than conquerors through
him who loved us. For I am convinced that neither death,
nor life, nor angels, nor rulers, nor things present, nor things
to come, nor powers, nor height, nor depth, nor anything else
in all creation, will be able to separate us from the love of God
in Christ Jesus our Lord."

Romans 8:31-35, 37-39 NRSV

I invite you now, during this season of Lent, to follow Jesus
all the way to the cross. Death is the doorway to life.

[1] Adapted from *A Treasury of Jewish Folklore,* edited by Nathan Ausubel,
New York: Crown Publishers, 1948, pp. 472-475.

Rev. Ryan Ahlgrim
First Mennonite Church, Indianapolis
Ash Wednesday Service
at St. Andrew Presbyterian Church
February 13, 2002

Ryan Ahlgrim graduated with a B.A. in English from Goshen College
and received his M.Div. from Associated Mennonite Biblical Seminary in
Elkhart, Indiana and his Doctor of Ministry degree from McCormick Theological Seminary as part of the Association of Chicago Theological Schools
D.Min. in Preaching program. He is the author of *Not as the Scribes: Jesus as*
a Model for Prophetic Preaching (Herald Press, 2002).

"WHAT DID HE DO WRONG?"

Blessed are those who are persecuted for righteousness,
sake, for theirs is the kingdom of heaven. Blessed are you when
people revile you and persecute you and utter all kinds of evil
against you falsely on my account. Rejoice and be glad, for
your reward is great in heaven, for in the same way they
persecuted the prophets who were before you.

Matthew 5:10-12

O Lord, help us to become masters of ourselves that we might
be the servants of others. Take our minds and think through them,
take our lips and speak through them and take our hearts and set
them on fire.

Amen.

A children's social worker who worked at a group home for
troubled children once told this story. She discovered that many
of the troubled children in her care had never been inside a church,
and they had a lot of questions about God and religion, so she
decided to take them to visit her church to talk with her priest.

She brought them inside a huge Roman Catholic cathedral and they walked down the center aisle in wide-eyed wonder as they looked at all the statues and stained glass windows. Eventually they came to the high altar and they looked up and saw a huge crucifix, a cross with Jesus nailed to it.

One little boy was transfixed when he saw Jesus on the cross and stood there staring at it for a long time. Eventually, he pointed to the crucifix and asked his teacher, "Who's that?"

His teacher replied, "That's Jesus."

The little boy looked at her earnestly and asked: "What did he do wrong?"

Obviously, this little boy thought that Jesus must have done something terribly wrong and was punished by being nailed to a cross. How would you answer that little boy's question? What exactly did Jesus do wrong to deserve such pain and punishment?

If I had been there I would have liked to tell that little boy that Jesus didn't do anything wrong; in fact Jesus did everything right! But because there is evil in the world, sometimes we suffer even when we do things right.

The truth is that Jesus did do everything right! Even if you don't believe that Jesus is Lord and Savior, if you look at his life objectively, you'll see a person who was a good man and lived a good life. Scriptures tell us that Jesus "went about doing good and healing all who were oppressed." (Acts 10:38)

Jesus went about telling people the Good News that the God who created this whole universe is a caring God who loves each of us unconditionally as loving parents love their children. Jesus demonstrated by his life and teachings how to love God with your whole being and love others as yourself. Jesus taught us that the meaning of life is found in trusting our lives into the hands of God and giving ourselves in loving service to care for the needs of others.

Jesus went about laying his healing hands on the sick and dying, on the blind and deaf, on the lame and the leper and making them whole. Jesus went about feeding the hungry and reaching out his arms to welcome the outcast and lonely.

By any objective measure, we'd have to admit that Jesus was a good man who went about doing good. He did the right thing with his life and he still suffered and died a painful death because evil is real in this world and opposes the good and the true.

It has been true throughout history that people who do the right and good thing in their life often suffer as a result of the good they do.

For example, President Abraham Lincoln did the right thing when he opposed slavery and freed those enslaved in this nation. He did the right thing when he waged Civil War to hold our country together when there were those who wanted to tear it apart. He did the right thing and yet he suffered for it; he was assassinated at the end of the Civil War.

One hundred years later Dr. Martin Luther King, Jr. did the right thing when he protested segregation and discriminatory laws against African-Americans and other ethnic minorities. We look back now and honor him for doing the right thing but we know he suffered for it. He, too, was killed for doing the right thing.

In more recent times, Nelson Mandella protested the apartheid laws in South Africa which held Africans in oppression for decades and he suffered for it. He spent twenty-seven years of his life in a South African jail because he did what was right. Eventually, he was released, vindicated and elected president of South Africa.

But the truth about life is that we may do good in this world and still suffer for doing it!

Sometimes we live with the assumption that if we are good people; if we are faithful to God and loving and generous to others, then we'll have a pleasant and easy life free from pain and suffering. But God never promises that. God only promises that we will never suffer alone; that God will always go through it with us. The truth is that being good and doing the right thing is never a guarantee against suffering and pain.

In fact, Jesus seems to expect that when you do good you'll suffer. In the beatitudes in the Sermon the Mount Jesus says,

> *Blessed are you when you suffer for doing what is right,*
> *for yours is the kingdom of Heaven . . . You should rejoice and*
> *be glad when you suffer for doing what is right for great is*
> *your reward with God.*

In other words: You do what is right; you may suffer for it but ultimately you'll be blessed by God.

Kent Keith has written a little book titled *Anyway—The Paradoxical Commandments.*

In it he writes:

> *People are illogical, unreasonable, and self-centered.*
> *Love them anyway*
> *If you do good, people will accuse you of selfish ulterior motives.*
> *Do good anyway*
> *If you are successful, you will win false friends and true enemies.*
> *Succeed anyway.*
> *The good you do today will be forgotten tomorrow.*
> *Do good anyway.*
> *Honesty and frankness make you vulnerable.*
> *Be honest and frank anyway.*

*The biggest men and women with the biggest ideas can be
shot down by the smallest men and women with the smallest
minds.*
Think big anyway.
People favor underdogs but follow only top dogs.
Fight for a few underdogs anyway.
What you spend years building may be destroyed overnight.
Build anyway.
People really need help but may attack you if you do help them.
Help people anyway.
*Give the world the best you have and you'll get kicked in the
teeth.*
Give the world the best you have anyway.

You see, in the final analysis, it is between you and God. It
was never between you and them anyway.

This quotation reminds us to do good even though others may
not appreciate it or may demean it or even make us suffer for it.
But do good anyway because it is ultimately only between God and
us. Ultimately we're accountable not to them but to God. And Jesus
says, "Rejoice and be glad for great is your reward in heaven."

On September 11, 2001, 3,000 people suffered for doing what
was right.

It was right for them to get up that morning and to go their
offices and fulfill their responsibilities and commitments to their
customers and their employers.

It was right for them to cook and serve meals to those who
came for breakfast in the Twin Towers restaurant and to clean the
building.

When the first plane crashed into one of the towers, it was
right for the firemen and policemen to rush into the burning

building to try to save the lives of those trapped there.

All of those people did the right thing and they suffered and died for it because evil is real.

Recently, I visited with a man whose wife worked in the World Trade Center and was at the level where the first plane hit and she was killed immediately. He had seen all the e-mail messages about how God inspired many people not to go to work that day or had made them late for work so they were spared from death. He asked: "Does this mean that God did not care for my wife who did get up and go to work that day and was killed in the terrorist attack?"

I shared with him that I believe that God's tears were the first to fall when his wife and all those others were killed so tragically. I told him that I believe that God cared for his wife and all the others because God is the creator and lover of all people. In fact, God loves us so much that God has given us freedom to decide how to live our lives and some people chose to turn their backs on the God of love and destroy those they dislike. But the truth about life is that when we suffer for doing right, we never suffer alone because God is suffering with us and is seeking to bring good out of every tragedy.

I believe that out of every crucifying experience in life, God is seeking to bring a resurrection just as he brought resurrection and new life for Jesus out of his crucifixion. So I have been asking myself: What is the resurrection that God is bringing out of the crucifixion we experienced on September 11, 2001? What is the good that God is bringing out of this tragedy?

I believe that all of those who lost their lives on September 11 are loved and embraced by their loving Creator. They discovered on that day that they are much more than just a physical body. They discovered that they are an eternal soul that nothing, not a terrorist attack, death, or anything else, can ultimately destroy. We believe that, at death, we simply leave our physical bodies behind and continue our life journey in the hands of God.

On September 12, the day after the disaster, a teacher in Pennsylvania asked her class of sixth grade students to draw a picture of their feelings about this tragedy. One little ten-year-old girl drew a big picture of Jesus with open arms above the Twin Towers with thousands of people ascending into his open, loving arms. Her picture says it all for me. The truth about life is that evil doesn't have the last word and we believe that even when we suffer for doing what is right we can "rejoice and be glad for great is your reward in heaven."

Another good thing that has come out of this tragedy is that it has caused millions of people to re-evaluate their lives and priorities. When people realized that their physical lives could be snuffed out in just a moment's notice, it makes them re-evaluate their relationship with God. People who have been solely focused on success and material wealth are starting to consider the role of faith and religion in their lives. In our congregation we have had a 30% increase in worship attendance in the year following 9/11. More and more people are asking the spiritual questions about the meaning of their lives. Out of this tragedy God is bringing something good in terms of new spiritual growth for millions of people.

Another blessing to come out of this tragedy is that people are beginning to spend more time with their families.

Ridgewood, New Jersey, is a suburban community of about 30,000 people just across the Hudson River from New York City. Twelve residents of Ridgewood lost their lives in the collapse of the Twin Towers. After the disaster, the people of this community began to re-evaluate their over-scheduled and over-busy lives and how little time most families were spending together. Consequently, on Tuesday, March 26, 2002, the people of Ridgewood declared a moratorium on meetings. They requested that no school, no church, no community group, no government group or any other group have any meetings on March 26 so that people could spend that one night with their families. They called it the Ridgewood Family Night project and many families who observed it reported that they had a family dinner for the first time in months and actually spent time having a meaningful conversation with other members of their families.

The hope is that this positive experience of family time together will inspire people to spend more time together with those who are most important to them. Out of this tragedy many people are making new decisions about spending more time with those they love most.

Out of the disaster of 9/11 more people are seeking to gain a better understanding of other religions.

In the past several months, I have been on several panel discussions with Muslim leaders, Jewish Rabbis and Christian pastors where we shared the similarities and differences among our religious traditions. We have also offered courses on World Religions and interviewed persons from a variety of religious traditions from the pulpit. This crisis has made us all realize how important it is for us to develop a greater appreciation and understanding of the various religious traditions in our world if we are to live together in harmony on this planet.

Six months after the 9/11 tragedy, New York turned on huge bright lights near where the Twin Towers stood. I was inspired when I first saw those lights brightening up the night sky because they reminded me that light does indeed overcome darkness and life does indeed overcome death. For me, they are a sign of the resurrection because they remind us that out of every crucifying experience in life, God is bringing a resurrection and new life.

Within the past year we have all experienced crucifixion. Some experienced the personal crucifixion of losing their lives or their loved ones. Others experienced the crucifixion of their businesses and professions. Many experienced the crucifixion of the feeling of safety and security in the world. But, as Christians, we know that crucifixion is not the last word. As Christians we know that God is bringing about resurrection and even now, we see signs of it.

Therefore, we can say with Jesus, "Blessed are you when you suffer for doing what is right . . . Rejoice and be glad for your reward is great with God."

Rev. M. Kent Millard, Senior Pastor
St. Luke's United Methodist Church
Indianapolis
Delivered March 31, 2002

St. Luke's is the largest United Methodist Church in Indiana with 5,000 members and 3,400 in worship attendance each Sunday in ten different worship services. Dr. Millard is a graduate of Dakota Wesleyan University, Boston University School of Theology and received his Doctor of Ministry degree from McCormick Theological Seminary in Chicago. He is the author of *Spiritual Gifts* and *Get Acquainted with Your Christian Faith* published by the United Methodist Publishing House. He is the co-author of *The Passion Driven Congregation* which will be published by the United Methodist Publishing House in the spring of 2003. He and his wife, Minnietta, have two children and six grandchildren.

LOOK UP AND LOOK AROUND

Luke 24:49-53

Life's possibilities seem endless in a college classroom. Perhaps you're thinking right now about that day when you continue your education. You can imagine being riveted to every word that issues from the mouth of the professor. Or perhaps sometimes you'll take an alternate course, and daydream.

I did both. Sometimes I took verbatim notes. Sometimes I would daydream. It was fun, back in the mid-1960s. On daydream days I found it to be especially exciting to sit in class and anticipate getting together with my friends at three o'clock in the lounge of our dormitory, Bishop Whipple Hall.

After class, I would usually show up fifteen minutes early, to get a good seat in the lounge. As the minutes went by one could question whether the old chairs and couches would be able to withstand the enormous number of students who were filing in to find a seat. Some late-comers always had to stand.

But then time would come. At precisely three o'clock we would end our pleasant conversations and become riveted to the blinking screen of the modest television sitting in the corner. Very much like a congregation of Easter Sunday Christians we would suddenly, with committed interest, focus our attention on a person who is more than a man. Yes, we had gathered to see a super-human person . . . Batman!

The Bishop Whipple Lounge would rock, and we would sing with our own POWS and THUDS and THUNKS and WACKS!

Super-humans and super-animals draw crowds. Superman, Wonder Woman and Mighty Mouse are magnetic. The extraordinary is very intense, captivating and miraculous.

In 1962, when Spider-Man first appeared in the pages of Amazing Fantasy #15, the interest in this superhuman was out of this world. For in a short time (also in 1962), Spider-Man had his own comic book series.

So today, forty years later, *Marvel Comics'* most popular superhero stars in his own spectacular feature film. Yes, Spider-Man brings a story of good and evil, love and cruelty, and awesome powers that become both a blessing and a curse.

This box office mania is seen in the life of Christ's Church. The Super Star called Jesus seems to shine and attract crowds two or three or even four times a year with the same super-human qualities. And He, of course, draws people into crowded sanctuaries across the world! People flock in to see "Super-Baby in a Manger!" And some even come back to see the sequel, "The Empty Tomb!" And then, instead of leaping tall buildings, we hear tonight that Jesus goes straight up! That's the Ascension, the event we commemorate this season. Life's possibilities really do seem endless.

So, young sisters and brothers in Christ, what's going on here with Jesus? And why is it that we have only a few crowded mega days in the life of the Church? Why do crowded sanctuaries become lonely echo chambers?

Because Spider-Man type adventures, which draw some people to church, are short-lived. For faith in and enthusiasm about God are not built on a spectacular, worldly event. That is the environment of Hollywood and Batman and Robin and Chickenman. Instead, faith (or trust) is built and nurtured on the Faith of the Apostles, given to us generation after generation by God Himself in the Mystical Body of Christ called the Church.

Father Roger Haight, a Jesuit priest and professor of historical and systematic theology, addresses this distinction in his book, *Jesus Symbol of God*. He says, "Resurrection faith today is not belief in an external miracle . . . Faith-hope in the resurrection is [given to us] through a Jesus who is represented in and through the Christian community in a variety of different ways." And so we can say over a period of time in the life of Christ's Church, that together we come to know through God's Word and the Sacraments that "Jesus reveals God as God truly is."

Belief in God is a gift. Together, we receive the gift. This is the reality tonight as you begin your lives in new ways in the Church.

So, can Superman really leap tall buildings? Can Batman always overcome the Penguin? Is that Super-Baby really God? Is the tomb empty? Did a carpenter's son really ascend so that He, who was one of us, now rules and continues to care for us?

Questions phrased in this way are spectacular, and the ensuing drama will draw crowds. But the spectacular brings doubts, and the lights dim, and the crowds dwindle.

In contrast, this is our prayer for you tonight:

Gracious Lord, through water and the Spirit you have made these men and women your own. You forgave them all their sins and brought them to newness of life. Continue to strengthen them with the Holy Spirit, and daily increase in them your gifts of grace: the spirit of wisdom and understanding, the spirit of counsel and might, the spirit of knowledge and the fear of the Lord, the spirit of joy in your presence. Give these people a new vision, and a new life, a new view of your world.

So when we focus on the great Feast of the Ascension tonight, we are confronted with the awkwardness of presenting the Mystery of the Church in material terms. One fairly common, stained-glass representation shows a pair of feet dangling out of a cloud while people are gathered on a hillside looking at Jesus' feet. Is this scene representative of what Luke is really trying to suggest?

It's a surprise when Luke says that the disciples are *glad* about the whole thing. "And they worshipped Him and returned to Jerusalem with great joy. . . ." So why weren't they grieving? Perhaps the answer for them and also for us is that we together in the Church finally understand Jesus this time. Perhaps, at last, we with the disciples trust who He is. That's the gift. That's the joy.

The Ascension celebrates the exalted Christ ruling the universe, all time and all space. It is Christ who was contained in a human life, bound by time and space, who returns to the point from where He started.

So in the Faith of the Apostles, the Ascension does not present us with a spatial problem. We don't have to answer the question, "Where did He go?" Instead, the Ascension brings to us a truth. Like the Incarnation, the Cross, the Resurrection, the Ascension assures us about what God is doing with us. For while we are still in the middle of our earthly existence, we are lifted into the realm of God.

That, I believe, is our source of joy. Look up and look around. Look at your brothers and sisters in Christ. Rejoice!

As the artist Corita Kent said:
To understand
Is to stand under
Which is to look up
Which is a good way
To understand.
Amen.

Rev. Leonard M. Jepson, parish pastor
First English Evangelical Lutheran Church (ELCA)
Mishawaka

Sermon delivered at The Cathedral of the Episcopal Diocese of Indianapolis, Ascension Day, May 9, 2002.

Educated at Concordia College, Moorhead, Minnesota, BA in 1966, and
Northwestern Lutheran Theological Seminary, St. Paul, Minnesota, M.Div.,
in 1970, Reverend Jepson had pastorates from Idaho to Minnesota, and Indiana (Kentuckiana) and Michiana. A people-person, Jepson has literally worn
his shoe-soles thin as a mission developer and neighborhood visitor.

FINDING ROOTS IN A ROOTLESS WORLD

If the dough offered as first fruits is holy, so is the whole lump; and if the root is holy, so are the branches. But if some of the branches were broken off, and you, a wild olive shoot, were grafted in their place to share the richness of the olive tree, do not boast over the branches. If you do boast, remember it is not you that support the root, but the root that supports you. You will say, "Branches were broken off so that I might be grafted in." That is true. They were broken off because of their unbelief, but you stand fast only through faith. So do not become proud, but stand in awe. For if God did not spare the natural branches, neither will he spare you. Note then the kindness and the severity of God: severity toward those who have fallen, but God's kindness to you, provided you continue in his kindness; otherwise you too will be cut off. And even if the others, if they do not persist in their unbelief, will be grafted in, for God has the power to graft them in again. For if you have been cut from what is by nature a wild olive tree and grafted, contrary to nature, into a cultivated olive tree, how much more will these natural branches be grafted back into their own olive tree. (RSV)   Romans 11:16-24

When I saw that the local newspaper advertised my sermon on page one of the Faith Section, I thought, "My gosh; now I have to preach a good sermon." So I went back and worked on it some more. I hope I don't disappoint you. Although I'm an Episcopalian, I've always admired the Presbyterian Church's strong tradition of great preaching with people like Peter Marshall, one of my early heroes. I was touched by the movie, *A Man Called Peter* at an early age. I also like Presbyterians because I married one who has blessed me with twenty years of a wonderful and happy marriage.

Like many college professors, I live far from where I grew up: about thirty years and nine-hundred and seventy-five miles to be exact. In the course of earning graduate degrees and pursuing an academic career, I moved around quite a bit. I felt for several years very rootless here in Indiana—with no relatives closer than Florida and not many chances to visit them. So feeling connected and rooted in a community became a concern of mine, especially after growing up in a family that had lived in the same town for five generations.

So how do you find roots in a rootless world? Someone told me that in the metropolitan Atlanta area, the majority of the residents are from outside of Georgia. In the metropolitan Washington area, where I've lived, I bet that eighty percent of the people grew up elsewhere. The obvious answer to feeling rooted in a rootless society is to get involved in a church. After all, that's what churches are for—to build communities of faith and brothers and sisters in Christ. And yet, it doesn't take us long to discover that churches can disappoint us; they aren't perfect and it's difficult to feel close to a group of people you may only see once a week. It's difficult enough to remember all of their names.

Some people from various Christian traditions, recognizing the obstacles that modern churches face in building close-knit communities, have chosen another path. These Christians have tried, with some success, to build intentional, residential communities of faith. The most notable Protestant examples are the Sojourners Community in Washington, D.C. and the Koinonea Community in Americus, Georgia, which is where Habitat for Humanity originated.

That isn't a choice or a calling for most of us, however. We have obligations and responsibilities here and careers that we can't simply uproot. I think part of the answer is the church, but it is mainly where we find the answer, and not the answer itself. I recall the discussion that went on among college students of my generation that went something like this: If Jesus is the answer, what is the question? Christians have sometimes been accused of answering questions that no one is asking and a simplistic statement like "Jesus is the answer" may be one of them. And so this morning I want to probe deeper. I love this passage from Romans that we heard today; it speaks to my life story and is one of my favorites.

Intriguing parallels exist between the spiritual and physical universes, which is why Jesus spoke so often in parables. He told a lot of stories about farmers and farming, giving us the parable of the sower, the wheat and the tares, the mustard seed and yeast, the rocky soil and the good soil, the vine and the branches, and the workers in the vineyard—all to teach spiritual lessons. Paul, in this passage, speaks of roots. So I want to build upon that metaphor because I think it speaks to our deepest needs for feeling connected to a deep source of meaning and strength beyond ourselves.

Paul compares the believer to a "wild olive shoot" that was grafted into a rich root of the olive tree. When we visited southern Spain four years ago, I recall seeing thousands of acres of olive trees as we took the train from the Mediterranean coast to

Madrid. The terrain is mountainous and rugged. I wondered how they picked and cultivated some olive trees because the slope around them was so steep. Olive trees require strong and rugged roots to survive in this terrain. Grafting one variety of fruit tree into the roots of another is common among fruit growers. Since my father grew oranges and grapefruit for a living, I know that many orange trees are grafted onto lemon tree roots when they are young. Lemon roots are more durable and sturdy and can withstand the cold better than natural orange tree roots.

This passage from Romans offers a remarkable metaphor for the way in which we are grafted into the body of Christ. Our natural roots are not strong enough, and so we need another root system. In Paul's words, we have been cut from what is by nature a wild olive tree and grafted into a cultivated olive tree.

In the Purdue Master Gardener course I took about three years ago, I learned that roots have four functions: anchor the plant or tree into the ground; absorb water and other nutrients from the ground; store food reserves that the plant can use later; and conduct foot nutrients to the upper parts of the plant.

Spiritual roots do the same. They anchor us in a tumultuous and stormy world and help us absorb nutrients: teaching, knowledge and wisdom from the church and other Christians that we need. They store up spiritual reserves upon which we can draw in times of trial and they conduct spiritual nutrients into other parts of our lives: the social, intellectual and psychological. In so doing, strong spiritual roots result in healthier lives.

I enjoy gardening and have always enjoyed the outdoors. Growing up around orange and grapefruit trees, I watched my father plant, graft and fertilize the trees and do the dozens of other tasks associated with farming. I would like to take the agricultural metaphor further. I want to give you five pieces of advice: start with the right kind of seeds; use proper nutrients; keep out the weeds; get plenty of light; and recognize that you need a time of dormancy.

First, start with the right kind of seeds. In the Purdue Master Gardener course, the county agent advised us to avoid cheap seeds. He said the most expensive seeds were usually the best investment because they produced the most healthy, disease-free plants. Beware of the five or ten-for-a-dollar packages of seed.

Selecting the right kind of seeds means reading the right kinds of books and magazines—positive and uplifting material that nourishes and strengthens our minds. It means reading the Bible every day. It means watching the right kinds of movies and television programs and avoiding the wrong kinds. It means associating with people who bring out the best in us and avoiding those people who don't. I've recognized the importance of positive thinking and trying to create a positive environment for myself in which to live and work.

There are many cheap seeds you can plant in your mind: seeds of lust or mindless entertainment. Millions of people waste their minds reading a horoscope every day or create fantasies of striking it rich by purchasing lottery tickets.

Even the right kinds of seeds do not produce immediate results. You might not tell the difference right away. But do natural seeds produce immediate results? Of course not. If you plant tomatoes or corn, you won't see the plant emerge from the ground for at least a week or two and it can take months to see the fruit. It takes five years for orange trees to produce their first fruits.

Second, get the proper nutrients. Bags of fertilizer have three numbers on them, something like "24, 10, 10" or "10, 25, 20." Those numbers represent the relative proportions of nitrogen, phosphorus and potassium. Plants need all three in different proportions at different times of year: lots of nitrogen in the spring and lots of phosphorus and potassium in the fall and winter. We need the same kind of balance of protein, carbohydrates, fats, fiber and other nutrients.

The spiritual life needs a variety of nutrients that are all part of a properly disciplined lifestyle. We need to be in church every Sunday to hear the word of God preached and taught. We need to pray every day and create time to reflect on our lives and put them in proper perspective. We need the discipline of study that comes through systematic participation in Bible study or Christian education. We need to be in fellowship with other Christians so that we receive the nurturing love that comes only from within the body of Christ. We need to be accountable to other Christians for what we say and do.

Third, keep out the weeds. I hate dandelions and I attack them with a passion. They create a challenging game I play with myself every spring—sort of like trying to keep the squirrel out of the bird feeder. Weeds steal nutrients from the plant; they hog the sunlight and the rain and prevent it from reaching the lawn or flower garden. Dag Hammarskjold, the former secretary general of the United Nations, wrote in his book *Markings* "You cannot reserve a plot for weeds in the garden of your mind."

A lot of weeds are growing in this social and intellectual climate. You cannot avoid them. That reminds me of the story of the Kentucky mountain man who went up to Cincinnati one weekend. He was walking around a seamy section of the city one night when a guy approached him and said, "Hey buddy; you want to buy some pornography?" The man said, "I don't think so; I don't own a pornograph so I wouldn't know what to do with it."

A few years ago I was using the Internet to try to find information on a Christian journalism competition called the Amy Awards. The search engine I was using turned up an X-rated pornographic site. It seems that it took the phrase "Amy awards" and located an Amy who had won some beauty contest. But you don't have to let the X-rated thoughts dwell in your mind. You can click the "close" or "stop" buttons. The best way to prevent an adulterous relationship is to never let the tempting thoughts enter your mind.

You can move on, and in the words of Paul, focus your thoughts on:

Whatever is true, whatever is honorable, whatever is pure, pleasing, commendable: if there is any excellence and anything worthy of praise, think about these things.

Fourth, get a lot of light. Even though roots lie underground, they won't grow if the plant doesn't get lots of light that it converts to oxygen and conducts to the root system. The reason that it's important to prune plants and trees is so that the rest of the tree can get sufficient sunlight. Light provides the energy needed for photosynthesis to occur.

Light and darkness are such common metaphors in the Bible that it's difficult to pick the best example. Paul writes in First Thessalonians: "You are not in darkness so that this day should surprise you like a thief. You are all sons of the light and sons of the day." Living in the light means we live in fellowship with other Christians and with one another. It means that we live as if we have nothing to hide. We do nothing, either habitually or occasionally, that we would be afraid for others to know about. Even non-Christian psychologists recognize the importance of a transparent life—one lived in openness and communication with those around us. It's essential for mental as well as spiritual health.

Fifth, don't fear the down time or a dormant phase in your spiritual life. Just as there are seasons of the year, there are seasons of the soul. No more than a tulip can bloom year round can we live in a constant spiritual spring. A dormant period of the soul can be a spiritual winter precipitated by death, tragedy or failure in our lives. Or it doesn't have to be precipitated by anything at all. It doesn't mean the spiritual roots are withering away. It simply means they are preparing themselves for the next cycle of growth. A spiritual winter often means that spring is not far away.

When we're young Christians, we often look for the quick fix. We envy those who give the inspiring "before and after" testimonies and wish we had a big story to tell. If you asked me to tell you the story of my conversion, I couldn't because it happened in very boring ways over a period of about a year. God doesn't always create quick fixes and instant results. That doesn't make him less real—to you or to me. Most of us blunder along making a little progress here, regressing a little there and making more progress in the next step forward.

I've taken this metaphor about as far as it goes. All metaphors, though they help teach a point, break down somewhere. Fortunately we are not like plants or trees in that they live according to predetermined laws of nature. We, as free humans, can make decisions that affect the outcome of our lives. We can make the wrong decisions, stupid decisions that shipwreck our lives or cause them to wither up and rot away. Make no mistake, millions of people do. Or we can make the right decisions, day in and day out, that result in deeply rooted and anchored lives.

Christianity requires a conscious decision to accept Jesus as the son of God and follow him—patterning our lives on his example and accepting his teachings as the way we ought to live. Unlike tulip bulbs and daffodils, Christians don't reproduce themselves. Each generation, each child and each adult has to make that decision all by himself.

How often have you heard this story? So-and-so becomes a celebrity, an athlete or movie star. Fill in your blank—Darrell Strawberry, Robert Downey, Judy Garland, Truman Capote. They have millions of dollars, five homes and their own fan clubs. Then you learn they've been arrested on drug charges or entered a rehab clinic. It's a familiar story with a simple cause. They have no roots; they haven't rooted their lives in the only foundation that matters; the only one that holds. Learn from their mistakes and make Jesus Christ your foundation and root your faith in him.

Oh God, your ocean is so vast and my ship is so small. Your world is so difficult and my strength is so little. The distractions are so tempting and my willpower is so weak. Throw out the lifeline—give me an anchor on which to hold, roots on which to grow, a foundation on which to build, a Savior in whom to trust. Allow him to carry me across the tumult of this ocean, the turmoil of this world, and the tribulations of this journey; so that when I arrive on the other side, he will say, "Well done, thy good and faithful servant."

Amen.

David E. Sumner
Delivered at St. Andrew Presbyterian Church
Muncie
July 15, 2001

David E. Sumner is a professor of journalism at Ball State University at Muncie, Indiana, and a lay member of Trinity Episcopal Church in Anderson, Indiana. Dr. Sumner has preached at Episcopal, Presbyterian, Methodist, Baptist, Assembly of God and Disciples of Christ churches. He has published articles in more than fifty newspapers and magazines and is the author of two books, including *The Episcopal Church's History 1945-1985*. He has a master of theology degree from the University of the South and a Ph.D. in communication from the University of Tennessee.

THE QUEST FOR HAPPINESS

Rosh Hashanah and Yom Kippur are unique among Jewish holy days in that they are not associated with any particular event in our people's history. They are at once the most universal of days and the most personal.

Rosh Hashanah is cosmic; it is called *Yom Harat Olam*, "the day when the world was created." Yom Kippur is a day of reflection and introspection, a day of *Heshbon Hanefesh*, "spiritual inventory," when we seek to "re-create" ourselves.

And so, tonight I do not want to talk about world events, Israel or anti-semitism, the economy or terrorism—not even about congregational fundraising. Tonight I want to talk about *you* and *me*, about each of us in our individuality and our mutuality, about the irreducibility of what it means to be a human being, what we call in Yiddish a *Mentsch*.

One of the most moving prayers of the liturgy of the High Holy Days is the *Unetane Tokef*. Its haunting melody captivates us with the refrain: "Who shall live and who shall die?" It invites us to consider the difference between being truly alive and merely existing.

The prayer reminds us of the precariousness and preciousness of life, of the fires, the floods, the storms, the devastating earthquakes, the cruel swords, real or imaginary, that threaten us; it has us confront the fires of ambition, the daggers of envy, the wild beasts of resentment, the noose of insecurity, which are part of our human condition.

But the prayer also proposes an antidote. It tells us that while there is to life a "reality principle" (catastrophe, accidents, illness) over which we have little control or determination, there is also an "ideality principle"—how we respond; how we transcend; how we challenge the challenge.

The *Unetane Tokef* prayer proposes three resources: *teshuva, tefilah* and *tzedaka*—repentance, prayer and social responsibility. These have the power to change the character of our lives.

Teshuva points inward. It is repentance. It means "turning," taking a second look, reassessing, changing. Many situations may be beyond our control, but that does not mean there is nothing we can do!

Judaism does not teach that we are irrevocably creatures of sin; but Judaism, on the other hand, does not deny that we are prone to sin. We are sinners! That is why we are here at this season.

Our tradition speaks of the *Yetzer Hara*—the sinful inclination. But above sin and error reigns the *Yetzer Hatov*—the good inclination, the power of repentance and the inexhaustible grace of God.

If *teshuva* is the look inward, *tefilah,* prayer (the second principle of the *Unetane Tokef*) is the vertical link, the look upward. Tefilah reminds us that we are not totally independent and self-reliant. It is born of the awareness that we do not have all the answers.

In *tefilah,* prayer, we turn to God, the ultimate resource, the authenticator, not of all that is, but of all that ought to be. Judaism teaches us that God is not just "someone out there," but a deep awareness "in here" that causes us to rejoice in the beauty and the goodness of the world, to revolt at the ugliness of evil and reject the disharmony of wrongdoing.

The third element of the *Unetane Tokef* is *tzedaka,* the horizontal, the outward look. *Tzedaka* is our term for duty and responsibility. *Tzedaka* is not elective; it is morally obligatory. It is not mere charity. It is responsibility. It is our tax for the privilege of being human, our call from individualism to collectivism, from self to community. The rabbis teach that in good times and in bad times *tzedaka* redeems.

And so in the midst of a world filled with anxiety and concern, in a time of escalating tensions and declining stock portfolios, these High Holy Days call each of us away from self-pity and self-interest to look outward, to arise to a higher standard, to be more humane; to be, in short, a *mentsch.*

What does it mean to be a *mentsch?* It means to take to heart the lessons of *teshuva, tefilah* and *tzedaka.* It means to combine the grandeur of being God's partner, with the humility of being mere dust and ashes.

It means to balance wants with needs, individuality with community. It means to remember in a world of "infectious greed" that ultimately the only thing we truly own is what we can freely give.

Leo Rosten, a contemporary Jewish author, says: "Neither wealth nor status nor success nor fame nor popularity qualify one to be a *mentsch.* The key [to being a *mentsch*] is character, rectitude, responsibility, generosity . . .." And I would add, "a sense of humor."

The *mentsch* is a person who helps losers feel like winners; who is more concerned with being there for others than with being number one. The *mentsch* is the person who knows that there is

glory in coming in second or third, or in just finishing the race—
even in trying one's best and not reaching the goal.

A mentsch realizes that failure in the pursuit of honest goals
is not a disgrace. Failure doesn't mean you're inferior; it means you're
not perfect. It doesn't mean you've wasted your time; it means you
have a reason to start over. Failure doesn't mean God has aban-
doned you. Yom Kippur confronts us with our fallibility and tells
us, "be a mentsch" even when you fail.

A mentsch is not a saint. Every mentsch comes replete with
human warts and scars. When God challenged Abraham to find
ten deserving people for whose merit Sodom and Gomorrah could
be saved, what God implied were not saints, but mentschen. For
lack of ten mentschen a society was destroyed.

Can we act as mentschen even when it appears that so much
of the world is in disarray? Will our children and grandchildren
remember us as mentschen?

My friend Marsha Nitza Jospe died of a debilitating disease
at the age of thirty-three. During her illness she kept a diary to
pass on her hopes and values to her children. She wrote:

> *I want you to be good Jews . . . good, honest people . . . .*
> *Happiness is a goal, but not something we must have*
> *every moment. That is not life.*

And so, at this highest season of the year we don't wish each
other a "*Happy* New Year" but a *Shanah Tovah*, "A *Good* New Year!"
It is not that we are adverse to happiness. We Jews believe in *simcha*,
times of happiness and celebration that punctuate life's days and
seasons. Judaism has an expanded vocabulary of joy; ours is a tradition that affirms physical pleasure and material blessings.

The rabbis teach that each of us will be held accountable before

God in the world to come for every opportunity for pleasure that came our way that we failed to seize. Yet, Judaism sees happiness not as an end in itself, but as a by-product of a good, harmonious, balanced, relational life.

Some of you may have seen recently a movie titled *Thirteen Conversations About One Thing*. Like the biblical book of Ecclesiastes, it is a series of dialogues about the elusive quest for happiness: about the unfairness of life; the fact that often things don't make sense; that we do not get what we deserve; that bad things do happen to good people and good things to bad people.

The movie suggests that happiness lies not in the grand scheme, the big pursuit, the frantic accumulation of things and power—but in the simple gesture, the daily kindness, the unexpected smile, the extended hand, the friendly wave.

Some weeks ago I visited a member of our congregation, a kind, patient gentleman who has been in and out of hospitals at least seven times this past year. I saw him sitting, for the first time in quite a while, eating a meager meal. I asked him how he was. He said, "I feel *wonderful* just to be able to sit up and walk a little!"

I was reminded that the little things, the daily blessings we take for granted, can become so special. That is why Jewish tradition counsels us to start each morning reciting *brakhot*, blessings, expressions of thanksgiving for the beginning of a new day and the awareness that it is graciously given to us.

The September 16, 2002, issue of *Newsweek* magazine dedicates its "Health" section to the "Science of Happiness." Happiness has now become the subject of scientific inquiry by psychologists.

Data show that while there is a genetic component, circumstances in life have little to do with the state of satisfaction or of happiness people experience. Religious involvement is an important component of joyful living. But health, wealth, good looks and status have little effect on what researchers call "subjective wellbeing" (i.e. happiness). Even paraplegics and lottery winners typically return to their customary dispositions about six months after they have adapted to their adversity or good fortune.

Studies show that wealth is no indicator of happiness. In America, real income has doubled since 1960—yet family breakups have also doubled, and depression multiplied ten fold.

Ultimately, "authentic happiness," researchers conclude, has to do with a certain management and discipline of life. It is about expectations, about outgrowing our obsessive concern with "how we feel" and focusing rather on trying to make life "meaningful." Beyond *pleasure* lies *gratification* or *contentment*, "the enduring fulfillment that comes from developing [our] strengths and putting them to positive use" (Seligman).

These "scientific" conclusions are not new. They are as ancient as Aristotle and the Bible.

Leo Rosten writes:

> *Ask American parents what they want most for their child. The chances are they will reply: "To be happy." What is the myth, "happiness," that has bamboozled so many of us? And what is this idiotic thing, "fun," which so many chase after? Where people once said "Good-bye," they now say, "Have fun."*

I know of nothing more demeaning than the frantic pursuit of "fun." No people are more miserable than those who seek desperate escapes from the self . . . who plunge into strenuous frivolity. Some say the word "fun" comes from the medieval English "fol" —meaning fool.

Rosten continues:

The purpose of life is not to be happy. The purpose of life is to matter, to be productive, to have it make some difference that you lived at all. Happiness, in the ancient, noble (biblical) sense, means self-fulfillment—and is given to those who use to the fullest whatever talents God or luck or fate bestowed upon them.

Happiness, to me, lies in stretching, to the farthest boundaries of which we are capable, the resources of the mind and heart.

The Jewish humorist and radio personality Sam Levenson used to recite a poem titled "All I Got Was Words."

When I was young and fancy free
My folks had no fine clothes for me,
All I got was words:

Gott Tsu danken (Thank God),
Got vet geben   (God will provide),
Zol men nor leben un gezunt zein (May we only live and be
                                                  healthy).

When I was wont to travel far
They didn't provide for me a car.
All I got was words:

Gey gezunt   (Go in good health),
Gey pamelech   (Go slowly),
Hob a glickliche reize (Have a successful trip).

I wanted to increase my knowledge,
But they couldn't send me to college.
All I got was words:

Hob Seichel   (Have good sense),
Zei nisht kein nar   (Do not be a fool)
Torah iz de beste schoirah (Torah is the best mer-
                      chandise).

The years have flown,
The world has turned,
Things I've gotten, things I've learned,
Yet I remember:

Zog dem emes   (Tell the truth),
Gib tisidokoh   (Give charity),
Hob rachmonus (Have compassion),
Zei a mentsch!   (Be a mentsch!).

All I got was words.

Words. During these High Holy Days we speak many words; we confess our personal contrition, we witness to our shared aspirations, we promise our commitments. Will these make a difference in our lives? Or will our *tefilah*, our prayers, be empty words; our *teshuva*, our repentance, a rhetoric not meant; our commitment to *tzedaka* a hopeless oath not acted upon?

Will we make Sabbaths for ourselves? Will we teach our children Torah? Will we be models of *Ma'asim Tovim* and *tzedaka*: deeds of loving kindness and acts of justice in a world turned upside down that clamors for rectification and reconciliation?

The beloved Rabbi Levi Yitzhak of Berditchev once saw a

man rushing down the street looking neither to the right nor to the left. He asked, "Why are you hurrying so?"

The man replied gaspingly, "I am pursuing my livelihood. I have to go review my stock portfolio."

"And how do you know," continued the rabbi, "that your livelihood is running ahead of you, so that you have to rush after it? Perhaps it is behind you, and all you need to do to find it is stand still for a while. Yet, here you are, running away from it instead. Stand still my friend, stand still. Take time; be a *mentsch!*"

Tonight, my dear congregants and friends, my advice is:

Stand still! Look at your spouse, your partner. Love her, love him, now; for who knows what tomorrow will bring?

Stand still! Are your parents still living? Are you faithful to them as they were to you?

Stand still! Look at your children. Take time to be part of their world. Share in their growth, for soon they will go their own way.

Stand still! Be a *mentsch*. Look at your friends. Tell them of your joys and pains; listen to theirs. To have a friend, one must be a friend.

Stand still! Tonight is Kol Nidre; tomorrow will be Neilah. Some gates will surely close. Make sure that others will open. Enjoy days filled with sunlight; tomorrows may be cloudy. Tomorrow the sun will rise, but we may not.

Who shall live and who shall die? Who will merely exist and who shall truly be alive? Who shall be a mentsch?

And so, I wish you:

Have a *good* and, in the end, also a *happy* New Year!

Rabbi Dennis Sasso
Congregation Beth-El Zedeck
Indianapolis
Kol Nidre 5763, September 15, 2002

Rabbi Dennis C. Sasso earned his Bachelor of Arts degree in Near Eastern and Judaic Studies at Brandeis University, and Master of Arts in Religion from Temple University. He has been rabbi of Congregation Beth-El Zedeck since 1977. He earned his Doctor of Ministry degree from Christian Theological Seminary in Indianapolis and holds honorary Doctorates of Divinity from the Reconstructionist Rabbinical College, Jewish Theological Seminary and Christian Theological Seminary. An author of many scholarly and popular articles on Jewish faith and cultures, he teaches at Christian Theological Seminary and Marian College.

YOU CAN RUN, BUT YOU CAN'T HIDE

Psalm 139

When you're little you "understand" Mister God. He sits up there on his throne, a golden one of course; he has got whiskers and a crown and everyone is singing hymns like mad to him. God is useful and useable. You can ask for things, he can strike your enemies deader than a doornail, and he is pretty good at putting hexes on the bully next door, like warts and things. Mister God is so "understandable," so useful and so useable, he is like some object, perhaps the most important object of all, but nevertheless an object—and absolutely understandable.

So begins "Anna's" description of our life with God in the delightful book *Mister God, This Is Anna!*
Anna continues:

Later on you "understand" him to be a bit different but you are still able to grasp what he is. Even though you understand him, he doesn't seem to understand you! He doesn't seem to understand that you simply must have a new bike,

*so your "understanding" of him changes a bit more. In what-
ever way or state you understand Mister God, so you diminish
his size. He becomes an understandable entity among other
understandable entities. So Mister God keeps on shedding
bits all the way through your life until the time comes when
you admit freely and honestly that you don't understand
Mister God at all.*

King David shares Anna's struggle. Psalm 139 appears to
express the struggle of David and God. We see the frustration, the
struggle, the embarrassment, but in the end David's point is this:
*Once we get in touch with this God who knows everything, goes ev-
erywhere, and has designed us, then we should change the way we live
our lives.*

This four-stanza poem takes us on a personal journey of
David's struggle with God.

I.

This journey begins in frustration at the all-knowing, suffocating *presence of* and *pursuit by* the creating God. God did not create
the world and walk away. No, God is alive and well and working
with this world. David discovers that God is a God of perception.
God knows you! *God knows me!*

*O LORD, you have searched me
and you know me.
You know when I sit and when I rise;
you perceive my thoughts from afar.
You discern my going out and my lying down;*

you are familiar with all my ways.
Before a word is on my tongue
you know it completely, O LORD.

Psalm 139: 1-4

There is no way to hide from God. As we read the first six verses of this psalm we sense David's frustration. David writes:

You hem me in—behind and before;
you have laid your hand upon me.
Such knowledge is too wonderful for me,
too lofty for me to attain.

Psalm 139: 5-6

In short, "God, you know too much. You're watching me everywhere I go. You know my every word. I'm suffocating here. I need a little space."

The question arises: What does God know about you that bugs you? What did you get away with this week? Was there some action that you felt a little guilty about? Some activity that you really wouldn't want anyone else to know of?

Isn't that why we don't like the all-knowing, all-seeing God? Maybe you got away with what you did. Maybe your spouse didn't find out. Maybe your boss didn't find out. But God saw it all.

O LORD, you have searched me
and you know me.
You know when I sit and when I rise;
you perceive my thoughts from afar.

II.

We try to run away. We pretend that God isn't there. We act as though there is no God. But David knew! David knew that God makes a difference. David was a colorful character. He knew how to live faithfully with God, but he knew how to sin as well. David once had a man killed not because he was angry with Uriah and not because Uriah had wronged him. NO! David had Uriah killed so that David could marry the man's wife!

God was disappointed in David. Actually, God was really angry to say the least. However, we discover a part of God in God's response to David. God did not get angry with David for having Uriah killed. God was angry not for what David did to the man, but for the offence against God. When dealing with you, God is not so concerned with what others do to you, as what you do to God. Others may hate you and hurt you. That gives you no reward. What God judges in you is the love that you extend in return. And not just on the outside, but the love you feel in your heart! David knew this when he wrote:

> *you perceive my thoughts from afar.*
> *. . . you are familiar with all my ways.*

III.

So, once we encounter God, we can't escape our God. God is always there. Our responsibility to live as God directs is always there. As David sang:

> *Where can I go from your Spirit?*
> *Where can I flee from your presence?*

If I go up to the heavens, you are there;
if I make my bed in the depths, you are there.
If I rise on the wings of the dawn,
if I settle on the far side of the sea,
even there your hand will guide me,
your right hand will hold me fast.
If I say, "Surely the darkness will hide me
and the light become night around me,"
even the darkness will not be dark to you;
the night will shine like the day,
for darkness is as light to you.

Psalm 139: 7-12

When I read these words, I think of Jonah. Jonah was called by God to go to Ninevah. Ninevah was the capital of a great and powerful nation. The Assyrians could and did invade and capture Israel. Yet God called Jonah to go to the king and tell him of God's love. Jonah was naturally scared to go to this great and powerful king. God called Jonah to go to the northeast. Jonah hopped on a boat going due west!

Jonah tried to run away from God, but he discovered that he could not escape God. Wherever he went, God was there. Even out on the sea far to the west God raised a storm, and Jonah was thrown into the sea. The story tells us that a great fish swallowed him and took Jonah back to the East Coast where Jonah was spit out onto the dry land.

God started over. "Go to Ninevah, Jonah." Off to Ninevah—reluctantly but faithfully—Jonah went. You see, when Jonah realized that he could not escape God's presence, he changed his mind. He did as God asked. *Once we get in touch with this God who knows everything, goes everywhere, and has designed us, then we should change the way we live our lives.*

By the time he gets to the third stanza (v.13) David's attitude reflects the fact that he must let God be God. Like Jonah, David considers the particular path of God's direction for him. Jonah and David discovered that our God is a God of purpose. *God built you and has a plan for you.* Spanish musician, Pablo Casals, once said: "The child must know that he is a miracle; that since the beginning of the world there hasn't been, and until the end of the world there will not be, another child like him."

> *For you created my inmost being;*
> *you knit me together in my mother's womb.*
> *I praise you because I am fearfully and wonderfully made;*
> *your works are wonderful,*
> *I know that full well.*

> *How precious to me are your thoughts, O God!*
> *How vast is the sum of them!*
> *Were I to count them,*
> *they would outnumber the grains of sand.*
> *When I awake,*
> *I am still with you.*

Psalm 139: 13-18

IV.

This psalm is a struggle for control of life. Will David win? Will God win? It begins in struggle and frustration but ends with wonder and praise.

Search me, O God, and know my heart;
test me and know my anxious thoughts.
See if there is any offensive way in me,
and lead me in the way everlasting.
Psalm 139: 23-24

Notice the verbs David uses: search . . . know . . . test . . . know . . . see . . . lead. In others words, "God, call me on the carpet." David has moved from *frustration at God's intrusion* into his life to *invitation of God* to freely see him as he is. David sees the flaw of his theology. He has been viewing God as an intrusive thief, not as a skillful helper and guide.

We really don't have the option of not being known, or not being accompanied, or not being designed, *it is just that now we are surrendering to God and inviting God to CHANGE US!* Jonah and David learned that you can run, but you can't hide from God. By surrendering to God we are saying, "I don't want to hide behind my need to control or my fear of my past or my pain in change." God looks at our life, finds the wrong and shows it to us, changes us, so that we're fully ready and focused to be used in God's glorious ministry. So relax. Like David, let God grow. Let God be a little bigger than you may have imagined when you came in this morning.

Rev. Gary M. Schaar
Associate Council Director, So. IN Conf. UMC
Preached at Old North UMC
Evansville
July 9, 2000

Gary M. Schaar is an Associate Council Director of the South Indiana Conference of the United Methodist Church. His principal responsibility is conflict management. Now in his twenty-first year as an elder, Gary has been choir director, associate pastor, or pastor in congregations throughout southern Indiana. Gary holds a B.A. in Music and Associated Studies from the University of Evansville and a M.Div. from Christian Theological Seminary in Indianapolis.

THE TOP 10 REASONS TO HAVE A *MARY* CHRISTMAS

Luke 1:26-35

When God determined to visit our planet, He could have followed virtually any path or pursued any one of a limitless number of strategies. What God ultimately chose to do was amazing. He risked everything on the response of a Jewish teenage girl who, if she were alive today, would have been taking final exams last week either in middle school or high school. God changed the world through Mary—which is why, with a nod to David Letterman, we now offer The Top 10 Reasons to Have a *Mary* Christmas this year. Let's get started.

Number 10   **Mary allowed God to mess up her life.**

Now, we could put it much more politely than that. We could say, "Mary was *available* for God's purposes." But the truth of the matter is that God thoroughly messed up her life. That, by the way, is something that God does all the time.

What did God ask Mary to do? He asked her to become

pregnant by the Holy Spirit so that she might be the mother of the Messiah. In other words, she was chosen. In the Bible, two things always accompany being chosen. One is a set of special privileges. The angel tells Mary that she has "found favor with God." Her relative Elizabeth will soon tell her that she is "blessed among women." But the other outcome of being chosen is terrible responsibility. Simeon the prophet will say to Mary, "A sword will pierce your soul." This was not exactly the life she had imagined for herself.

Nothing has changed after 2,000 years. When given permission, God still messes up the modest dreams of ordinary people so that extraordinary things might happen through them. How did Mary respond to God? She was actively passive. "Here I am," she said. "God, you are now free to interrupt my life as you see fit." Here's a question worth asking ourselves during any lulls in the action over the next twenty-four hours: Does God currently have permission to interrupt *me*?

Number 9   **Mary listened to God.**

That's not as easy as it sounds. Most people in most generations have organized their lives so as *not* to be able to hear the voice of God. We tend to favor distractions—sports, media, appointments, "busyness," vacations, our oh-so-urgent lists of things to accomplish. It's no accident that right from the top the angel Gabriel says to Mary, "Don't be afraid." There are exactly three-hundred-sixty-five "Don't be afraids" in the Bible—conveniently, one for every day of the year. God, after all, has a reputation of messing up people's lives. So who wants to listen to God?

Mary did. Medieval scholars fancifully came to the conclusion that the organ of conception in Mary was her *ear*. Tonight, the most important thing we might hear from God is what she heard from the very beginning: since God's in charge of everything going on in our lives right now, we don't have to be afraid.

Number 8　　**Mary restores our faith in teenage role models.**

We don't know how old Mary and Joseph were when they became engaged, but it's likely that neither of them would have met the minimum requirements for obtaining a driver's license in Indiana. The preferred future of every young woman in first century Israel was marriage and motherhood, so it wasn't unusual for engagement to begin at age thirteen. Adults usually didn't live longer than forty years, and the average city dweller died at the age of twenty-nine. Thus, even though Mary and Joseph were young, they had to be prepared to make life-changing decisions.

Women in the ancient world weren't exactly valued for their brains. Some rabbis even said that teaching a girl was a waste of time. Women were thought incapable of significant spiritual insights. But Mary had the last laugh. She listened to God. Her flesh became God's flesh. None of the wisest men over at the temple could ever have fathomed *that*.

Interestingly, in our own time we have come to know several self-professed celebrity "teenage virgins." They tend to generate both popular music and parental anxiety. It's a joy, therefore, to recommend an alternative teenage role model. Her name is Mary.

Number 7　　**Mary Chose to Lose the Honor Game**

The Honor Game is played in every century, in every culture. The only thing that changes is the way we keep score. Americans tend to compare possessions: What kinds of toys are under your Christmas tree? What species of SUV is that sitting in your driveway? Where did you get that sweater?

The classic version of the Honor Game, however, concerns relationships. What matters is the significance or the scandal of the company you are keeping. Are friends and strangers alike convinced that you are cool—a person worth knowing and being seen with? How did you ever get a date with *him*? Why do you lower yourself by being seen with *her*?

In the ancient world public honor was unquestionably the most valuable commodity. Preserving one's own reputation and the honor of the family name was Job One. Mary knew what she getting by marrying Joseph, a man of the "house and line of David," Israel's most famous king. She was inheriting a name of great worth. Mary also knew what it meant to say yes to the angel Gabriel. She was losing everything. Pregnant and unmarried? The whispering campaign would begin overnight and it would never end, not as long as she lived. *She had a boyfriend on the side.* Mary's honor would evaporate.

About the time that Joseph saw Mary trying on maternity clothes, he had a wrenching decision to make. In an effort to spare her as much humiliation as possible, he decided to terminate their engagement out of the public eye. That's when God said to him, "Joseph, wait. Mary is blameless here. I'm the one who has messed up her life. Come to think of it, Joseph, I'd like permission to mess up yours as well."

God asked Joseph and Mary to lose the Honor Game. From the moment they said yes, people never fully understood the truth of their situation. Not only that, they then began spending time with all the wrong people. Pagan astrologers showed up talking about a star. Shepherds came to the delivery room. Keep in mind that people who tended sheep for a living occupied the lowest rung of Israel's social ladder. This would be like flagging down the local garbagemen and saying, "How would you guys like to come into the house for a while? You can sit in our family room and take turns holding our new baby."

Losing the Honor Game means that we care more about what God thinks about our possessions and our relationships than what other people think.

The truth is that we cannot love and try to be cool at the same time.

Number 6   **The real Mary is much more interesting than Hallmark.**

Generations of Christmas plays and Christmas cards have dulled our senses to the fact that Mary was a real person. She was not an icon or an image. Almost certainly she never wore the blue robe in which she is most often portrayed. It was hard to come by blue and purple dye in the first century. Hundreds of little seashells had to be processed in order to produce a tiny amount of purple, which is why it became the color of kings.

When it came time for Mary's ritual of purification at the temple following Jesus' birth, she and Joseph presented two little birds for the sacrifice instead of a lamb. That's clear evidence that they were poor. We don't know if Mary rode a donkey all the way from Nazareth to Bethlehem, as most Christmas cards imply. But if you've ever been in the final trimester of a pregnancy, would you really have begged for the opportunity to ride a donkey for eighty miles?

Luke tells us that the newborn Jesus was laid in a manger, a feeding trough for animals, because there was no room for them in the *kataluma*. That Greek word has traditionally been translated "inn," but it's much more likely that *kataluma* means "guest room." Since Bethlehem was a town long settled by David's family tree, Joseph and his expectant fiancee would undoubtedly have been welcomed into the home of an extended family member—apparently a house with a small *kataluma*, or guest room, off to one side. That space already being filled, Mary probably gave birth in the central part of the house.

To this day many Middle Eastern homes are split-levels. People live in the upper part, while animals come in and out of the lower level. At night the goats and cows are brought into the house for their own security, and to provide warmth for the humans. You could say that kind of heat is measured in BTUs—Bovine Thermal Units. Many homes would have had a chiseled, stone manger available for the animals. Add some handfuls of clean straw, and Mary had a warm place to lay her son. She was a real person who lived at a real moment of real history.

Number 5   **Mary didn't live down to her name.**

Her parents named her *Mara*, which in Hebrew means "bitter." Apparently something sad or painful had accompanied Mary's birth. As she grew older she certainly had reason to become bitter. Her reputation was shot. In all likelihood she buried her husband, because he never appears in the gospel accounts after we encounter Jesus at age twelve. She was agonizingly present at the public lynching of her firstborn son. But Mary refused to live out the negative implications of her name, which is why "Mary" has become one of the warmest, most revered names in the world.

Somewhere along the way, did somebody hang a painful name on you? Was it a teasing sibling, or a cruel parent, or an unfeeling kid on the playground, or somebody who betrayed your trust? We all have a choice. We can either live down to our painful names or nicknames, or we can use them as lifelong reminders of God's grace, forgiveness and love.

Number 4   **Mary didn't flinch at the impossible.**

During the angel's visit she has just one question. It's not, "Why me?" or "Why now?" or "Can you guarantee that everything's going to work out?" Instead, Mary asks something very practical. "Since I'm a virgin," she says, "how is this going to happen?"

Gabriel's answer is poetic. "The Holy Spirit will come upon you, and the power of the Most High will overshadow you." He summarizes, "For nothing is impossible with God." That's not a particularly detailed answer. It's certainly not a theological or technological explanation. But it's the one thing Mary needs to hear. Even if she doesn't have all the answers, God can be trusted.

Number 3   **Mary took on the role of a Servant.**

The final words of her encounter with Gabriel are astonishing. Mary says, "I am the Lord's servant. May it be to me as you have said." She identifies herself as God's *doulos,* which means "servant" or "slave." Today we can hardly imagine calling ourselves slaves and feeling that we have made a healthy decision. But in Bible times things were different.

Slaves made up one third of the population of the Mediterranean world. Another third of the people were former slaves. In Israel slavery was a common arrangement to pay off debts. By law I might be forced to become a member of your household and be under your authority. But the Old Testament specifies that at the end of seven years, I would have to be set free, no matter how much money I owed you. Perhaps, however, you've treated me well. Perhaps being a member of your household has blessed me. Therefore if you and I are in agreement, I can choose to stay under your authority as a bondservant.

How would that happen? I would stand by your front door, and put my ear right against the wood. Then you would take an awl—essentially, an ice pick—and push a hole right through the cartilage of my ear. That mark would signify that I have chosen to become a lifelong servant in your household.

That was Mary's choice. "Lord, here I am. You're now in charge of my life. I am your servant." That can be our choice, too.

Number 2   **Mary treasured up all these things in her heart.**

What Luke tells us is that after Mary hears the amazing story told by the shepherds—what they heard and experienced out in the fields—she captures those memories and makes treasures out of them. Some of us sleepwalk through even the most important moments of our lives. Mary, however, is captivated by a sense of wonder.

When I was a teenage couch potato, sprawled across the living room sofa watching TV, my mom would occasionally sit down near my feet and sigh deeply. "Oh, honey," she would say, looking at my size eleven sneakers. "I remember when I could hold both of your little feet in the palm of one hand." That was always a bit embarrassing, especially if I had a couple of friends sitting there.

Now that my own kids are teenagers, and I look down at their size thirteen sneakers, I know what my mom was feeling. She was feeling a sense of awe. She was wondering, "Where did the years go? How did this happen so fast?" Mary made treasures out of the irreplaceable moments of her life. Are we committed to do the same? Are we grimly trying to do everything we can just to survive the next few days, or are we asking God to kindle in us a transforming sense of wonder?

And finally, the Number One reason to have a Mary Christmas this year:

Mary said yes to God, with no strings attached.

When it comes to relating to God, America's most popular game is *Let's Make a Deal*. But God didn't come to negotiate with Mary. He didn't offer terms. God came to claim the life of a young woman. "From the beginning of the universe," he said, "I have known this day would come. Now . . . will you let me do this? Will you put your future into my hands?"

Because Mary said yes, we're sitting here tonight. If at this moment your heart is stirred—stirred by the possibility of what might happen if *you* really did it—if *you* really said, "God, here I am, your servant . . . and my reputation and my relationships and my future belong to you"—then know without doubt that God is still in the business of choosing people, setting before them special privileges and terrible responsibilities. Will you say yes to that . . . no strings attached?

Rev. Glenn W. McDonald
Zionsville Presbyterian Church
Zionsville
Delivered Christmas Eve, 2001

Glenn McDonald is senior pastor of Zionsville Presbyterian Church, a congregation he helped establish in 1983. He holds a degree in biology from Purdue University and an M.Div. from Trinity Evangelical Divinity School in Deerfield, Illinois. He is an avid spelunker and amateur astronomer. In 2000 Zionsville Pres was identified as one of the "300 outstanding Protestant churches" in the United States.

Don't Give Your Heart
to the Church

Text: Revelation 21:10; 22 - 22:5

However one experiences something depends a great deal on the perspective one has during that experience. In baseball, the pitcher and the catcher and the batter are all part of the same event, but because of their particular perspectives their experiences are different. And, of course, the infielders and the outfielders and the coach and the fans are all part of the same event but their own experiences are all different.

Over the last fifteen years the perspective from which I have participated in the life of the church is that of a pastor. On forty-eight out of fifty-two Sunday mornings every year I find myself standing in the pulpit instead of sitting in a pew. And in regard to the life of the church the perspective of the pulpit has both advantages and disadvantages. The church has been the source of some of the most beautiful things I have ever seen in life. I can't begin to tell you the number of people I've visited over the years, people who are in the midst of a major crisis—an illness, a death, a personal struggle, but what that they have testified to the love of the church. Invariably, wherever I go to offer my care I am able to follow the footsteps of Christians who have already been there—

sending a card, writing a note, bringing food, sending flowers. Folks, don't ever say, "Well all I can do is . . . "—for the things you may think are so little, so inconsequential, are the very acts of care that keep many hearts going. I've been there. They've shown me the cards, told me you came by to visit, said there was so much food they didn't know what to do. There are times when from my perspective the church is beautiful and it bears witness so well to the God of love and care whom we believe in.

The church has also provided me, just to be honest with you, a continually flowing river of laughter. Just like in a lot of your families where when you get together you laugh until your sides hurt, I get so tickled at some of the things that happen in church life that I have trouble breathing. I'll never forget the Sunday when I was preaching in another congregation, when in the middle of the sermon, I heard this loud noise. A woman in the church had fallen asleep while I was preaching and had slumped forward and smacked her head on the pew in front of her. She shook my hand on the way out of the church that morning and as I noticed the red mark across her forehead she said, "Mark that was the best sermon you've preached in a long time."

Bulletin bloopers are also an endless sort of laughter. These are a couple of classic ones:

> On Wednesday the Ladies Society will meet. Mrs. Johnson will sing "Put Me in My Bed" accompanied by the Pastor.

> This afternoon there will be a meeting in the south and north ends of the church. Children will be baptized at both ends.

Beauty and laughter, I see them both from my perspective in the church. Yet, sadly I see all too often from this perspective ugliness and bitterness as well. I've seen Christian folk treat one another in some of the most cruel and spiteful ways imaginable. I've seen people grab for power in the church because they couldn't get power anywhere else and once they have power run over everyone else because they were in charge. I've had people in the church who didn't get their way come in and talk to me and tell me that they would do everything they could to get their way and everything included "gettin' rid" of me. I had a colleague who wrote in a letter once:

> It is sometimes ridiculous to take the church seriously as an adult institution. Does everyone come to church to be coddled? If they don't agree with what the church is doing they resort to blackmail by saying they will just quit giving. And how immature some people are expecting the pastor to show up on their door step and take their side every time there is even the slightest conflict.
>
> I sometimes laugh at what the people are missing in church, because if I don't, I'll spend all my time crying.

And, of course, it's not just conflicts at the local level that are troublesome. The church is fragmented in so many different ways. Right within walking distance here we have five different congregations, all seeking to do our own thing. Think about what a witness it would be if we all became one congregation—seven hundred strong in worship, all sorts of strong programs we could run, instead of everyone limping along, everybody doing the same. Could you imagine trying to preside over a meeting in which these five congregations tried to become one? Jesus prayed that all who believe in him would be one even as he and his Father are one, but we are far, far from that.

Then there are the times when segments of the church have simply opposed the movement of God's spirit and the Gospel's call of justice for all. The Civil Rights movement in America was at the same time maybe the American church's finest hour and saddest witness. The Christian spiritual strength of many was what undergirded the civil rights movements and I am proud that that movement was led by a man who considered himself first and foremost a preacher. But at the same time there were white Christian congregations in the south and the north, in the east and the west, who were taking votes that said they as a congregation would not integrate, black people would not be welcome to worship the God who made us all.

And history has shown us as well that a contributing factor to the Jewish Holocaust of WW II was Christian anti-Semitism. And while our Jewish brothers and sisters and their children were being murdered too much of the church remained silent. And now in ecumenical circles apologies to the Jewish people are being issued by various denominations on a regular basis.

So from my vantage point, as a pastor, a preacher, a student of the Christian faith, I see the beauty, I experience the laughter, and I wince at our sin. And with all that I've experienced and from the perspective that I do experience it, I have to be honest with you. As much as I love the church and even though I plan to spend the next thirty years or more seeing things from this particular perspective, just to be honest with you, I have not given my heart to the church. I have not given my heart to the church.

Now that may sound like a strange thing for the pastor to say, "I haven't given my heart to the church," but I believe that if I'm going to be faithful and honest as a pastor, I have to say that and even more. I have to say to you, "Please, don't give the church your heart." You see, I think we should save our heart for that which is Ultimate, for that in which beauty reaches its holiest heights and in which ugliness doesn't reside at all. And the church isn't the Ultimate.

The text for this sermon is from the book of Revelation, John is getting a picture of what the final consummation will be like, the day when God redeems all of heaven and earth. And in this final consummation, John bears witness to the Ultimate. He says, "I saw no temple in the city, for its temple is the Lord God Almighty." You see, the Temple represented the faith for the Jewish people, it held God's very presence. Remember that one of the charges against Jesus was that he said that he would destroy the temple, the very thing that represented their faith. But here is John saying that there would come a day when there would be no temple—"for the temple will be the Lord God Almighty."

John says that the Ultimate is not the temple, it's not the church, the Ultimate is God. The church isn't the ultimate, the church bears witness to the one who is the Ultimate; the one who is not only light but the source of all light. The church tells God's story which goes from eternity to eternity, a story of which we are only a part. We tell of God's purposes for all of creation to know holiness and righteousness, to walk in fellowship with the divine.

To give our heart to the One who is the ultimate is to give our heart to the one who welcomes all who wish to come, while the church too often argues about who is welcome. To give our heart to the Ultimate One is to give our heart to the one in whom all racial and ethnic barriers are broken down and a new humanity exists in that oneness. To give our heart to the One who is ultimate is to give our heart to the one in whom no evil dwells, the

One in whom evil is out of place. Though the church has great beauty at times, the church also has been the harbinger of things that are less than beautiful—prejudice, denial of truth, betrayal, deceit, abuse of power—sometimes these evils creep into holy places. But they do not creep into the One who is holy.

If you give your heart to the institutional church, thinking that the church is the-all-in-all, the ultimate—you will be disappointed. And if we, as the church, ask people to give us their heart we will be leading them in the wrong direction. What we need to invite people to do is to give their heart to God, the God we know most fully in Jesus Christ. There is nothing more vital to accomplishing the mission God has given us—which is to bear witness to the ways of heaven's kingdom, the way of blessing and life—than for us to have hearts devoted not to ourselves but to the One who is the ultimate source of all that is and ever will be.

About John's words in Revelation, the theologian Karl Barth wrote: "Nothing is more finally significant than the church's complete absence. No place of worship, no temple, synagogue or church building is needed any longer—because there is God." God is the Ultimate and it is to God that I encourage all of you to give your heart.

Hearts that are committed first to God will help keep the church on track, for when we get tempted to keep everything just the way it is because that's what makes us comfortable—we will remember the God who makes all things new, the God who pokes and prods and disrupts moving us ever onward from living in complacency toward a fuller expression of justice and righteousness and love.

Hearts that are committed first to God will help keep the church on track, because when we start thinking that being a Christian and coming to church is all about the clothes you wear and the prayers you pray and how much you put in the offering plate and who you run around with, we remember the God who said through the prophets that he desires more than anything else kindness and mercy and humility. We remember the God revealed in Jesus Christ who said to the religious folk of his day, if you are worried about the outward appearances while the inside is being neglected you better change your focus—you better quit worrying about the clothes everybody's wearing and worry about clothing your own heart in love. And may we always remember that Jesus was particular about who hung around with. He made sure he was always surrounded by sinners who needed love.

Hearts that are committed first to God will help keep the church on track and we need that, because, brothers and sisters, it's easy for the church to get off of the track. And it's those hearts committed to the Ultimate source of all that is and ever will be that will straighten us out if we dare to listen.

The fact is, brothers and sisters, commitment to the institutional church, to its form and structures, is in a great decline. The generation that is now being raised does not have the same level of commitment to the institutions, that the previous generation did. In many Christian circles such a change in institutional commitment is decried. It is said that there is something wrong with the new generation and their level of commitment. But I will not say that. In fact, what I say is this:

The changing focus of commitment may well be a blessing from God, for God is reminding us that the church is not the ultimate, and surely then no form or structure that the church has taken over the last 2,000 years is the ultimate. God is reminding us that our work is not to get people to give their heart to the church, our work is to invite people to give their heart to God.

From my perspective as a leader in the church, the church is at times beautiful, the church is a source of great joy, but the only true way I can be a leader in this body is not to give it my heart. I'm trying my hardest to give my heart to God. That's where I encourage you to give yours.

Mark E. Poindexter, Pastor
First Christian Church
Salem
Delivered May 20, 2001

Mark E. Poindexter was ordained into the ministry of the Christian Church (Disciples of Christ) in December of 1990. He received his Master of Divinity degree from Emmanuel School of Religion in Johnston City, Tennessee. His Doctor of Ministry came from Christian Theological Seminary in Indianapolis. Dr. Poindexter has served as a volunteer Hospice chaplain, a church camp counselor and is founding president of the local Habitat for Humanity affiliate. He enjoys family camping with his wife, Becky, and their two children, Christopher and Michele.

KEEPING THE MAIN THING
THE MAIN THING

One of the teachers of religion who was standing there listening to the discussion realized that Jesus had answered well. So he asked, "Of all the commandments, which is the most important?"

Jesus replied, "The one that says, 'Hear, O Israel! The Lord our God is the one and only God.

And you must love him with all your heart and soul and mind and strength.'

"The second is: 'you must love others as much as yourself.' No other commandments are greater than these."

The teacher of religion replied, "Sir, you have spoken a true word in saying that there is only one God and no other.

And I know it is far more important to love him with all my heart and understanding and strength, and to love others as myself, than to offer all kinds of sacrifices on the altar of the Temple."

Realizing this man's understanding, Jesus said to him, "you are not far from the Kingdom of God." And after that, no one dared ask him any more questions.

Mark 12:28-34 (LB)

In John Eldredge's beautiful book, *Wild at Heart,* he says: "Have you thought about God's handling of the Gospel? God needs to get a message out to the human race, without which they will perish forever. What's the plan? First, God starts with the most unlikely group ever: a couple of prostitutes, a few fishermen with no better than a second grade education and a tax collector. Then He passes the ball to us. Unbelievable!"

In our text, Jesus gives us the essence of the Gospel we must pass on. Here the Master spoke with a group of religious teachers about the real meaning of Deuteronomy 6:4, 5. This passage is called the *shema* in Hebrew which basically called for believers to do two things: "Love God and love people the way you want to be loved." That is the Gospel in miniature. Jesus said in essence: "That's it!" That's the main thing! On those two laws hang all the laws and the prophets. Love God and love people: nothing more, nothing less, and nothing else. It is what I call "keeping the main thing the main thing."

It should be the focus of our faith. It is the only hope for a nation that has lost its way. Someone has said that our future as a civilization depends not on the "love of power but the power of love." Jonathan Edwards of old said: "We have just enough religion to hate, but not enough to love." Max Lucado, our contemporary , has said: "God loves us just the way we are, but He loves us too much to leave us like that." Dr. Martin Luther King, Jr., an apostle of love, said it best: "We must learn to live together as brothers or we will perish as fools." In other words, keep the main thing the main thing. It's the key to our survival but even more important it is what we must pass on and pass down to our children.

Our text speaks for itself in outlining at least three things we must realize:

First, love has to be the *first* thing.
Secondly, love has to be the *one* thing.
Finally, love must be *our* thing.

I. First, love has to be the first thing.

Verses 28 and 29 in Mark 12 are a clarion call to put "first things first" and keep the main thing the main thing. Listen as the scribes ask the Master "which is the first commandment of all?" Jesus answers: "The Lord God is One Lord and you should love the Lord with all that is within you: your mind, soul, and strength of spirit. This is the *first* commandment."

There are one thousand different definitions of love and yet the scriptures declare decisively in one thousand different ways that God is love. It is one statement that bears no successful contradiction. The Apostle Paul says that "all things work by love." The God of the Judeo-Christian faith is not some Aristotelian unmoved mover who passively ponders himself. Oh, no, our God is a personal God of love and a God who cares for all of His children equally and excellently. As the praise and worship chorus says:

Our God is an Awesome God.
He reigns from heaven above.
With wisdom, power and love
Our God is an Awesome God.

This idea is the only hope we have in a world now divided by religious totalitarianism. What else but the universal realization that God is One and God is love can serve as an antidote for the poison of religious bigotry? What else could heal the insanity that allowed Muslim fanatics on September 11, 2001, to finger prayer beads while they slammed passenger plane bombs into the World Trade Center with the shout "Allah Akbar" meaning in Arabic, "God is great?" Now before we become too self-righteous, let us not forget that we as a so-called Christian nation with a so-called Christian president declare war on sovereign nations without legitimate or just cause and kill the innocent in the Name of God. In World War II, it was called, "praise the Lord and pass the ammunition." Today, the cry is "praise the Lord and save the oil." Either way, it is a perversion of the purpose for which we were created. We were born to love and not to hate. As the slogan goes: We were born to "make love not war." We must learn to even love our enemies. Jesus said: "love your enemies, bless them that curse you, and pray for them that despitefully use you." He said to every potential Peter. "Put up your sword. History is replete with the bleached bones of nations that fail to follow this command."

The first thing must be *one* thing.

In Verse 31 of our text, Jesus says:
And the second is like the first—the same as the first—you must love your neighbor like you want to be loved. Nothing is greater than these two—love God with all you've got and love others the way you want to be loved. Jesus says in essence that they are the same.

In other words, *two* things are really just *one* thing. Loving God is inextricably bound to loving people. Here is where the Jews and too many of us have our problem.

Our problem is not in belief but in practice. You see these ancient Jews recited the *shema* daily, but the problem was that it *only* applied to Jews. This is not what Jesus had in mind. Jesus took the discourse to another level by saying in essence that loving God is inextricably bound to loving your neighbor the way you want to be loved. Not only were these two things one, but Jews could no longer love God and just Jews, but they had to include everybody: Samaritans, Cyrenians, lepers, prostitutes, Palestinians *and* Jews. Yes, we too are called to love policeman, politicians, republicans, democrats, Iranians, Iraqis, Koreans South and North. Jesus said in essence, "we have to love black, brown, yellow, red and white because they are all precious in His sight." Love God with everything that is within you and love everybody the way you want to be loved. When we keep this charge as the main thing, it changes us and then we change the world.

How do you explain attacking another country without the heads of those countries sitting down and reasoning together first? Love demands a conversation. Love expects a conversion. We are not commanded to agree but we are commanded to love.

The race problem in America will not be resolved until we see loving God and loving people the way each of us want to be loved. We must love people—all people—as the same thing. We must redefine "neighbor" not as those who merely look like us, think like us, or even live next to us. Our neighbor is anyone that Christ died for and He died for the whole world.

Dr. King has said so appropriately: "We have through our technological genius made this world a neighborhood. We must now through our moral genius make this world a brotherhood." It serves no purpose to arrogantly strut through the neighborhood of nations as a big bully when you know that "what you sow you shall also reap."

One of the highlights of my ministry is an example of what we have to do to adhere to the Master's mandate. For years, in the city of Indianapolis, a brother begged for a living at the corner of Keystone and 86th Street, one of the city's busiest intersections. He would stand at the end of the exit ramp with a sign that said, "will work for food." He was there for years. Many passed him by. Some gave money but most would not even look at him. Some gave him a "please don't ask me for anything because I gave at the office" look. One day after having given him all three responses, I decided to love him. I rolled down my window and asked him if he really wanted a job, I would find one. I gave him my telephone number and the address of our church. I didn't hear from him for five years. Then one day in worship, as I customarily issued an invitation to discipleship, I asked if there was anyone who wanted a new life and if they did, I wanted them to meet new Life Himself, Jesus Christ. From the back of the church came a small man whose pock-marked face was familiar. This was the same man with the sign and the "beg." The same one so many ignored. He said that many had given money and many had looked away in disdain or changed lanes to avoid him, but no one gave him their phone number and offered a job. This man is now a member of our church and a worker on the construction site of our new building. When I say "I love you and there is nothing you can do about it," I mean it. Sometimes you have to love the *hell* out of people. Love brought this brother all the way back. It's what happens when you keep the main thing the main thing. My grandmother taught me not to turn my back on a stranger because it could be the Prince of Peace in disguise.

Finally, not only must love be the *first* thing, and the *one* thing, but it must be *our* thing. We must own it. We must take responsibility for love. This is what Jesus had in mind when he explained to the scribe what it takes to get into the Kingdom of God. In verses 32 through 34, the scribe indicates agreement but not action. Jesus said in essence that belief without practice like faith without works is dead. The scribe said, "I believe that the Lord God is one Lord and that we should love God with everything we have and love our neighbor like we love ourselves." He agreed that this is the main thing and supercedes anything else. And Jesus says in verse 34 in response to the scribe's statement of agreement: "You are not far from the Kingdom of God." Then the Bible says "after that no man dare ask him any questions." Why? Because Jesus gave us the bottom line if we want to get into the Kingdom of God. Put your faith into action! Love somebody back to life. Forgive an enemy and make them your friend. Forgiveness is at the heart of love. Revenge is at the heart of hate. Max Lucado says it this way: "Forgiveness does not mean the other person is right. It just means you are free." It starts with a renewed mind and can be detected through common courtesy. The Bible asks: How can we love God whom we have not seen and hate our neighbor whom we see every day." In other words, how can we say we love God and not even speak to or smile at the person sitting next to us in the pew? As one man said in a fit of honesty: "I love humanity, it's people I can't stand!"

Keep the main thing the main thing. It has to be the *first* thing, the *one* thing, and ultimately *your* thing if you are going to change the world—even your world.

As I close, let me share a little of my story. In my book, *Mama's Boy*, I tell my story. It is a love story. It's my story, but you will surely find yourself in it. It is the story of how a rejected boy becomes a respected man of God. It is the story of how pain fuels passion. I am convinced that "God does not waste an ounce of our pain nor a drop of our tears" without using you or somebody to fashion faith out of failure, hope out of hurt, and promise out of pain.

You see, I am a *Mama's Boy*—Mrs. Marilla Roberts Jackson's only grandson—spoiled and made special by grandma's hands. She knew how to make the main thing the main thing. Have you ever been touched by grandma's hands? Many of you had the luxury of being raised in a nuclear family, but that's not my story. My experience was not nuclear, it was unclear. I knew what it felt like to be "dissed" like the biblical Joseph and dropped like the biblical Mephibosheth. My name was as Jabez. I was born in pain.

My parents divorced when I was only five years old. They took me to then famous St. Louis Union Train Station. They put me on a train by myself. They said they didn't want me anymore. I was only five years old. They were sending me to my grandmother in Cleveland, but they never told me I had a one-way ticket. They said, "Tommy, you'll be all right. We have asked this nice porter to take care of you." And they gave me over to a stranger. I was only five years old. He had the shiniest gold buttons, skin like ebony, and teeth like ivory. He was nice to me and put me in the upper berth of a sleeper car for an all night ride to Cleveland. All night long, the train snaked its way through Illinois into Ohio, clickety clack, clickety clack, clickety clack until early the next morning it pulled into the then famous Cleveland Terminal Tower Train Station. The porter dressed me. I had on my little shorts, two-toned oxfords, and sailor cap. The porter said: "do you see your grandma?" and at first, I could not because of the steam. I almost panicked, and then as if she stepped out of the cloud, there she was, all five feet of her with her little hat, her little worn coat, and a smile that could light up the darkness.

The porter put me in his arms and took me to the steps. He set me down and put those portable steps down, went back up the steps, got me, and there was grandma's hands. I jumped into her arms, and she hugged me crying, and I was crying, and she said, "How's Mama's boy?" *Love alive* on the train platform. When I jumped into her arms, I jumped into the arms of Jesus. Her love brought me back to life. She kept the main thing the main thing.

I believe George McCleod was right when he said:

I simply argue that the cross be raised again in the marketplace as well as the steeple of the church. For Christ was not crucified on a communion table between two candles, but on a cross between two thieves, on a town garbage heap where cynics curse and men talk smut. This is where He died, and this is what He died about. This is where we should be, and this is what we should be about. Love: nothing more, nothing less, and nothing else.

Keep the main thing the main thing.

I cannot speak for you, but I still am lifted by the words to that old hymn:

Love lifted me. Love lifted me.
When everything else had failed, love lifted me.

Rev. Tom Garrott Benjamin, Jr. Senior Pastor
Light of the World Christian Church
Indianapolis

Tom Benjamin has been the Senior Pastor of the historic Light of the World Christian Church (Disciples of Christ), Indianapolis, Indiana, for the last thirty-three years. He is the fourth senior pastor in the 136-year history of the church. Under his leadership, Light of the World Christian Church has consistently been one of the fastest growing churches among the Christian Church (Disciples of Christ).

Earning his undergraduate degree from St. Louis University (B.A.), he holds two graduate degrees, M.Div. and D.Min. from Christian Theological Seminary, Indianapolis.

In February 2001, Light of the World Christian Church was recognized as one of the "best of the best" among three hundred excellent Protestant congregations across the United States by an independent national study at the University of North Carolina at Wilmington.

Bishop Benjamin's passion is children, and he has authored three books: *Boys to Men*, *The Home Alone Syndrome*, and his most recent book, *Mama's Boy*.

NINEVEH OR BUST

During the westward movement of the 1800s many pioneers would paint a slogan such as "California or Bust" on their wagons. I suppose it was an effort not just to announce to others, but to remind themselves of their destination—it's a little harder to get sidetracked and abandon your course once you've committed yourself in public. Perhaps it gave them the determination to carry on to "gird up [their] loins" as the scriptures say, and prepare themselves for the perils that lay ahead.

Perhaps it was also a cry for fellowship and a call for fellow pioneers, with similar destinations, to band together with them in unity. We all need the fellowship of other believers in our lives, to strengthen our resolve to keep walking toward our eternal goal.

The trail west was fraught with mountains and plains, hiding snakes, robbers and the months of frustration and work. Most of us can barely imagine the commitment it took for these pioneers to make it through to the coast.

As our pioneer ancestors held their slogan of "California or Bust" out for all to see, I propose that we today adapt a slogan that will serve us wherever we go in life as we apply its greater meaning to our daily struggles. That slogan is *Nineveh or Bust!* Turn with me, if you will, to the story of Jonah in the Bible.

> *Now the word of the Lord came unto Jonah the son of*
> *Amittai saying, Arise, go to Nineveh, that great city, and cry*
> *against it, . . . But Jonah rose up to flee unto Tarshish from*
> *the presence of the Lord . . .*
>
> Jonah 1:1

Jonah received a call he did not want, a call he would not even take. He offered his own objection. Ah, those *buts* . . . always get in the way don't they. *But* I don't have the money . . . *but* I don't have the time . . . *but* I want to watch TV. Here at the prison, we are divided into numerous dorms. There are some 1700 inmates. Plans are, by this summer, to add another 1500 or so to our population. We are the size of a small town. Yet we are in fact, a microcosm of our greater American upbringing. Some of us come from large cities. Others come from rural areas. Still others of us come from foreign countries or are first generation Americans. My own ancestors were Irish and German. The Becks, the Geyers and the Druckamillers were among the first settlers in Indiana. The Becks came up through Kentucky, where they lived for a time. My great-great-great grandfather, Simeon Beck, came to Indiana around 1819, teaching school near Richmond, Indiana in 1822. Later he and his family moved north. I read with amazement the account of their move from North Manchester to Goshen, Indiana. Today the trip would take about an hour and fifteen minutes by car. Then, it took them three days. Not long after their arrival in Elkhart County, Simeon died leaving his wife, Mary, and their older children struggling to survive in this new and foreign environment.

Certainly many of us are in a new and foreign environment here. Many of us had never known the inside of prison walls until recently. This is my first incarceration and I am determined it will be my last, yet it is possible to look at this time as a blessing from a loving and caring God. That is not because we want to do time. It is not even because we believe that this is the best alternative for sentencing. Rather, it is because we believe God is working in our lives, to use this time for a greater good. To develop within us qualities that we can use to better our lives, and not to get us into the old patterns of behavior that resulted in our crimes. All too often however, we, like Jonah, are full of *buts*. We must make our own trip against our will to our own Nineveh. We must confront the problems in our lives, which led us here.

Not only did Jonah have objections, but he also had the audacity to "flee from the presence of the Lord." Now none of us would ever do that, would we? Perhaps we can learn a little something from old Jonah.

Seriously, we say we want to go to Heaven, to enjoy the Lord's presence, to praise him, but do we really? To be in the Lord's presence takes work because the Lord is always on the front lines of the battle. We must fight our way to the front if we would be with Him. Rev. 3:21 says: "To him that overcometh I will grant to sit with me in my throne, even as I also overcame, and am set down with my father in his throne." *So fleeing won't work.* We have to set out on that journey and not run away.

> . . . *and he went down to Joppa; and he found a ship going to Tarshish: so he paid the fare thereof, and he went down into it, to go with them unto Tarshish from the presence of the Lord . . .*

The scriptures use the word *down* twice in just three verses . . . whenever we are fleeing from the presence of the Lord, it will always bring us *down*. Jonah was busy fleeing . . . *but* the Lord had other plans.

> *But the Lord sent out a great wind into the sea, and there was a mighty tempest in the sea, so that the ship was like to be broken.*
>
> Verse 4

You see, those ships that we take to flee, won't endure. When the sea gets to beating and bashing them around, we are likely to be broken. **We cannot run. We must accept and endure.**

That reminds me of Matthew 7:24-27,

> *Therefore whosoever heareth these saying of mine, and doeth them, I will liken him unto a wise man, which build his house upon a rock: And the rain descended, and the floods came, and the winds blew, and beat upon that house; and it fell not; for it was founded upon a rock. And every one that heareth these sayings of mine, and doeth them not, shall be likened unto a foolish man, which built his house upon the sand; And the rain descended, and the floods came, and the winds blew, and beat upon the house; and it fell: and great was the fall of it.*

You see, Jonah, like many of us, wanted that house on shifting sand, he wanted to go to Cancun, Mexico rather than Juneau, Alaska . . . and he was about to be *broken*.

> *Then the mariners were afraid and cried every man to his god, and cast forth the wares that were in the ship into*

the sea, to lighten it of them. But Jonah was gone down into
the sides of the ship; and he lay and was fast asleep.
Verse 5

. . . fast asleep; that happens when we are content to live in
sin and are unwilling to change—when we have fled from God's
presence. We fall fast asleep—we would rather dream, than to hear
and follow God's call.

I have a confession to make . . . I don't really like it here . . . I
don't want to be in prison. I want to be home with my family.
Frankly, there are times when I would rather be almost anywhere
but here. Apparently however, this is where the Lord wants me,
at least for now.

So the shipmaster came to him, and said unto him,
"What meanest thou, O sleeper? Arise and call upon thy God,
if so be that God will think upon us, that we perish not."
Verse 6

What did he mean by "O sleeper"? He was calling Jonah to
repentance. Jonah was caught sleeping when he should have been
working for the Lord in Nineveh.

Skipping down to verse 12, Jonah tells them:

Take me up, and cast me forth into the sea; so shall the sea
be calm unto you: for I know that for my sake this great tem-
pest is upon you.

Jonah couldn't run far enough from the Lord, so now he's going
to try and get someone else to do the dirty work for him, "If I can't
run from the Lord, I'll just die," was what he was saying—yeah right,

that will help! Death always gets us away from the call to the Lord—
Jonah wasn't too smart, was he? Maybe we can learn something
from him anyway.

Jonah finally convinced them to do what he thought would
get him out of a bad situation. They threw him overboard.

> *Now the Lord had prepared a great fish to swallow*
> *Jonah. And Jonah was in the belly of the fish three days and*
> *three nights.*
>
> Verse 17

After Jonah had a bit of time to think . . . he gets vomited out,
onto the shore and the Lord calls him again:

> *Arise, go unto Nineveh, that great city, and preach unto*
> *it the preaching that I bid thee. So Jonah arose, and went* [to
> the place he should have been in the first place] *unto*
> *Nineveh, according to the word of the Lord*
>
> Jonah 3: 2-3

I have a friend, a Baptist minister, with whom I have been
corresponding for some time now. He is one of the few people in
my life that I have been able to be completely honest with, and he
still accepts and understands me even though he may not always
agree with me. In a recent letter, he said that he has come to think
of prisons as modern day monasteries. I really like that idea. I have
often thought about this time as almost a second mission for me.
I was privileged to be able to serve a two-year mission for my church
in Mexico, from 1977-1979. There I developed a great love for the
Hispanic people. I have also developed a great love for some of my
brothers I have met here in prison. The idea of a monastery where

you can reflect on life and where you fit in the grand scheme of things is very appealing to me. Too many of us have been busy our whole lives chasing a living and we have forgotten what real living is about.

We have been swallowed up, unawakened. And the temptation goes on to ignore the voice of God. Even here, where we have the opportunity to put concentrated daily effort into our relationship with God—apart from the daily pressures of earning a living, which we knew on the streets—sometimes, I'm afraid we allow ourselves to occupy the whole day doing things that are of no lasting benefit . . . like watching TV. In the large day rooms in our dorms, some people exercise, some spend their time playing cards or other games, some study school work, some talk on the phone—if they can afford it—and some study the scriptures.

I confess—I have become quite a TV-aholic. Like many of you I purchased a TV for my cell and I find myself spending hours in relative seclusion in front of the tube . . . far more that I ever did when I was free. Recently I find I have had to force myself to shut the thing off and go out into the day room and get to know other people, or to just sit quietly and meditate on how the whole of God's word really applies to me personally and how I can best serve my fellow men. I have found that when I get quiet, I am better able to hear what the Lord has to say to me. That is often a challenge even in the best of circumstances.

The road to Nineveh is noisy with many distractions that can divert our attentions. It seems we live in a constant flurry of activity. Those who aren't busy at other things often stand along the upper level of the cell house walkway visiting or yelling across the room at one another. Even standing next to one another, some people feel they can't communicate unless the whole room can hear. When we are locked in our cells at night, there is the constant jumble of talk on the guard's radio, inmate workers picking up and delivering laundry, or washing machines screeching to a halt between loads.

I formerly had a position as the scheduling clerk in the law library, here at the facility. My original intent in taking that position was to be sure I could get to the library each day to do my own legal work and to help others get there as well. (Perhaps that's the "control freak" part of my personality coming through.) As time went on, I allowed myself to become more and more frustrated. I am trying to hold the legal system accountable for the promises they made to me, and those guaranteed by law. This too can be a discouraging and all-absorbing pursuit. I got caught in a cycle that made it difficult for me to attain that monastery effect that my friend spoke about. In order to achieve that monastery mentality we may have to get swallowed up in silence, and that's why I'm thankful that the job as the Chaplain's clerk came along.

I appreciate the Chaplain for the many hours he spends on our behalf, and for his sense of humor. I appreciate the solitude and the opportunity for reflection that this position brings. Although there is still much to be done on a daily basis, there are quiet times when even as I work, I can reflect on my next step toward my Nineveh. In a recent interview, the comedian Jim Carrey said, "You have to pick up the mantle, whatever you are, you have to pick it up and wear it well. There is a price to be paid—a check for denial. It is not important to me to hang on to what I have, but to hang on to *who* I am."

I hope all of us, brethren, can hang on to who we really are as brothers and children to the most high God. I hope that each of us will take time as the New Year approaches to reflect on our own individual path to Nineveh. So I say to you today . . . *Nineveh or Bust!*

Go there of your own free will—don't make the Lord keep you treading water. I have to ask myself, as I ask each of you . . . how long will you spend in the belly of the fish before you go to Nineveh? Why Nineveh? Because that is where you will find the presence of the Lord. Why Nineveh? Because any other destination will leave us treading water or in the belly (swallowed) of a great fish.

Now therefore fear the Lord and serve him in sincerity and in truth: and put away the gods which your fathers served on the other side of the flood, and in Egypt; and serve ye the Lord. And if it seem evil unto you to serve the Lord, choose you this day whom ye will serve; . . . but as for me and my house, we will serve the Lord.

Joshua 24:14-15

I bear you my testimony that God lives. That Jesus is the Christ, that God takes a personal interest in each and every one of His children and that He knows what is best for us. We can spend years running, but true happiness can only be found when we accept the challenge of our own Nineveh.

Michael L. Harris, Chaplain's Clerk
Miami Correctional Facility
Bunker Hill

Michael L. Harris was serving as the Chaplain's Clerk, at Miami Correctional Facility at Bunker Hill, at the time this sermon was given. The congregation was interdenominational and primarily Protestant. Harris himself is a Latter-day Saint.

Harris holds an undergraduate degree in Theatre and Social Work. He completed numerous courses in writing and religious studies during his incarceration. He was released from prison in November, 2002, and is currently pursuing a career in video production and writing. Through his professional efforts he hopes to share his conviction of the need for positive prison reform and its relationship to our personal testimonies of the gospel of Jesus Christ.